THE END OF WORK

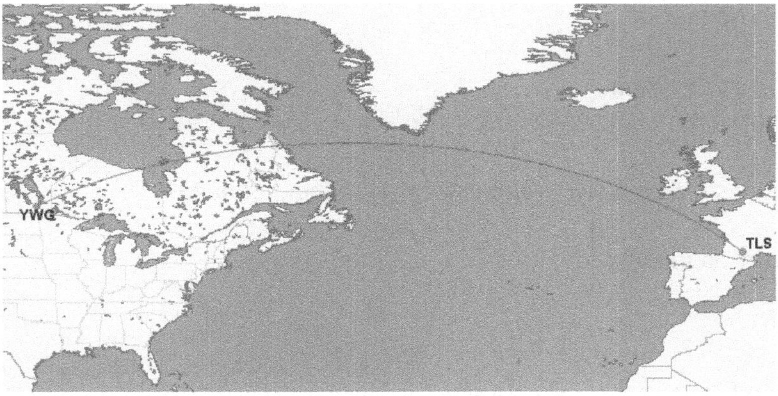

Financial Planning

For People

With Better Things to Do

Second Edition
ISBN 9781928169512

Published by *Navigator Services*, Winnipeg, Canada

Printed in Canada

Disclaimer: Material contained in this book carries no guarantee of any kind, express or implied. The author does not endorse, recommend or control linked websites and accepts no responsibility whatsoever for their contents, views or currency of information. Neither is the author recommending any particular investments. Any references to funds or stocks are only as examples of the point being made. Anyone seeking financial advice or services should consult a professional.

Is this your financial plan?

"If we take a late retirement and an early death, we'll just squeak by."

- The New Yorker

This tome is dedicated to my family, the most important investment anyone can make. I can't claim to have been good at it, but I sure have been lucky.

If you are curious about the "map" on the title page, that is the great circle route from home in Winnipeg to Toulouse in the south of France, my fantasy "End of Work" destination. Even our fantasies need a Plan!

*"Where Are the Customers' Yachts?"**

A visitor to New York was admiring the yachts that Wall Street brokers bought with money received for financial advice. He asked: "Where were the customers' yachts?" Of course, there were none. There is far more money in *providing* financial advice than there is in *receiving* financial advice. High fees are justified by the complexity of finance: *you could not possibly manage money on your own.*

You know you need to save and invest towards financial independence, to "end work" on your terms. You know you should protect yourself and your loved ones in case your work ends prematurely, by death or disability. Both goals require you to spend money on financial products. Up to now, you have had two choices:

1. You could trust a financial advisor to always have your best interest in his recommendations, and so do your financial planning on blind faith; or

2. You could become a DIY financial planner, spending enormous effort and energy, and making a lot of mistakes.

Before choosing, or continuing, with option 1, you may want to watch CBC Marketplace's

http://www.cbc.ca/marketplace/episodes/2013-2014/show-me-the-money.

My friend Don did option 2. He gave up on financial advisors twenty years ago, and started doing it himself, using the early discount brokerages and index funds. He wrote a book about it: "Don't Sell Yourself Short" in which he explained the rudiments of investing for DIYs. Of course Don had an MBA in Finance and did the Canadian Securities Course just for fun. He really enjoys the stuff. For those interested enough in finance to do-it-yourself, the bookstores and libraries have shelves of books. And "do it yourself financial planning" got 5,930,000 hits on Google in .35 seconds. There is no shortage of information. The only shortage is your precious time.

Now you have a third choice. You can invest in your *financial literacy* with this book. This option is for people who are not satisfied with option 1, but do not really want to pursue option 2 because you do have better things to do with your precious time. With option 3 you will still need to use the services of financial professionals but a modest degree of financial literacy will make you a more knowledgeable buyer of financial services. You will be better able to smell a rat, when the greatest thing since sliced bread is being pitched. And you may even be able to tell when you are getting your money's worth from the fees you pay for money management.

You may have been ripped off by today's financial industry. Or you may just be frustrated because you do not even know if you are being ripped-off. Or the whole subject of financial planning may be so intimidating you would rather spend time with the Devil. Better yet I suggest, is to learn the Devil's language.

So give me a couple of hours of your time. I am going to tell you about how the financial planning business works, and explain the basic products you will need to ensure your financial security. Then you can get back to your better things to do, or at least to a good book that you do want to read.

* Used by Fred Schwed Jr. in the title of his 1940 book on investing - *la plus ca change ...*

If you don't know what you want to do, it's harder to do it.

– Malcolm Forbes

What this book is about

Nobody can go back and start a new beginning, but anyone can start today and make a new ending.

-- Maria Robinson

The Big Picture

Financial literacy

Financial literacy can ensure that you only buy the protection you need – the least amount of insurance for the shortest time, but enough to cover your real needs that you cannot afford to cover yourself. And the basics of investing are really quite simple when you understand the fundamentals. The essence of financial literacy is in knowing enough, to have confidence enough, to be able to take responsibility for your own financial decisions. That is the purpose of this book.

This knowledge begins with an understanding of the financial advice business.

Advisor or salesman?

If your priorities for your time and energy do not include DIY financial planning, then you will still need to interact with financial advisors to pursue your financial goals. There are many financial planners and advisors who are knowledgeable and dedicated and really do care about their clients. Unfortunately, there are more who are not. There are some 90,000 people in the financial business across Canada. Most are paid on commission. They have to be pushy, and sell you whatever they can. It is a tough business in which to make a living, resulting in high turnover. A thick skin is required to get past the negative predispositions that resist a call from any salesman. Some financial companies recruit anyone with a pulse, sell them the "opportunity" to get rich, teach them some basic sales pitches, and then let them loose on you. Many have little financial background and may know less than you, but they have bought into the company sales pitch and can make their product sound "so-ooo" good. You may have already met one of these. There is no regulation of the term "financial advisor" or its variations. Anyone can hang out their shingle as a financial planner, once they meet the basic licensing requirements to actually sell financial products.

Only about one in three "financial advisors" is in financial planning as a vocation, to build a professional practice. These belong to a professional association such as Advocis, subscribe to a code of ethics, carry errors & omissions insurance and are committed to continuing education. When you do get a sales approach, you can screen if they may be worth your time by asking if they meet these basic professional standards. The good ones will also have some extra letters after their name, degrees in commerce or economics, or designations such as CFP for certified financial planner or CLU for chartered life underwriter, certifications that take several years of study and experience. Once you have found a professional, versus a "salesman", and have developed a relationship, hang on to them, and listen to what they have to say. The Advocis website will even help you find one at:
http://www.advocis.ca/secure/form/findanadvisor/profile.aspx

The financial professional's role is to consult with you in helping you understand the risks and alternatives to manage them. But only you can best decide your needs and priorities. Once gaps and needs are agreed, she can advise you on the best products and companies to match your needs and priorities.

What about regulations?

You may think the Big Brother of government regulations is going to protect you from unscrupulous salesmen. There are some fifty agencies, federally and in all the provinces and territories, which are "protecting" you as a financial consumer. Each province has their own regulatory agency for each of insurance and securities. A main function is to license sales people. An aspiring financial planner will need to pass the **LLQP** (Life License Qualification Program) and be supervised by a licensed agent for their first year. Annual license renewal does require continuing education credits that are obtained by attending financial company sales seminars. A similar exam and license is required to sell mutual funds and other investment products.

These regulatory requirements do ensure the consumer that even the "salesmen" in the business do meet a basic knowledge requirement. These exams are not easy and the study material is comprehensive. At least you will know that when you are oversold inappropriate products, the salesman did have some idea what he was doing! In short, regulation is a hodge-podge of agencies working in their own narrow silos.

To take an example, regulations require an advisor to complete your risk profile, to keep it in his file to demonstrate the product he has sold you is appropriate. The trouble is that everyone wants "aggressive" returns with "conservative" risks. This regulation suggests that you can choose to be one or the other. More likely, you will need some of each in a balanced portfolio. A psychological profile would be more useful. If you panic at each dip in the market, so that you always sell low after you had waited to buy high, conventional wisdom suggests you should avoid equity investments. Instead, you may just need some education about what is "normal" through a business cycle. Since you have better things to do anyway, do not even look at share prices from one annual review to the next.

Regulators cannot protect you if you choose option one. If you decide to put this book back on the shelf and be a sheep, you are sure to get fleeced, whatever the regulations. Take responsibility for your own choices and it will be a lot harder for the school yard bully to take advantage of you.

And you may have to do more on your own anyway. In the interest of consumer protection and disclosure, the U.K. and Australia have banned embedded compensation (they mean commissions; transparency would be helped by plain English) and have imposed a *statutory fiduciary duty* obligation. Similar regulatory changes are now being proposed in the U.S. and Canada. CRM2 rules, effective July 1st, and just being seen by many clients in their yearend statements, do require more disclosure from financial advisers, such as reporting their charges in absolute dollars instead of just a percentage. The satire shows are already spoofing poor clients trying to make sense of these new disclosures. On the down side, under such regulations in the U.K., some 25% of advisors left the business due to the costs of compliance, including all the paperwork to prove fiduciary duty. That cost forces the rest to focus on higher net worth clients, where more revenue on larger sales can compensate for the added cost of the regulatory compliance. That can leave the rest of us relying on Google for our financial advice.

Advocis is advocating a “professions model” of regulation, where financial advisors would be regulated in the same way as accountants and lawyers. That would be a big help, having a professional body that could impose real sanctions on the “salesmen” of the financial world. But would it really offer you protection? Think of the recent expose on the wrist slapping received by lawyers from their self-regulator for embezzling their clients’ funds

Only you have the big picture

The value proposition in using an independent financial advisor is that they can take a holistic view of your needs. In practice, financial advisors tend to specialize in the protection side (insurance products) or the money side (investment products).. There is more money to be made in the money side. Both sides are complex and require the advisor to invest time and effort in knowing the products, as well as in developing their sales skills to keep eating. The majority will be too busy trying to make a living to really be an expert in all the products available. Your advisor may have been giving good advice on the money side, but has she been neglecting your needs on the protection side? Only you have the truly holistic picture of your own needs.

This book explains risk management for your income during your earning years and risk management for your investments that will provide your income after your Work Ends. It hopes to make you more confident as a buyer of the financial products which will protect you from a premature End of Work, as well as provide your income for the rest of your life after you choose to End Work.

Having a degree of financial literacy will actually make you a more attractive client to the truly professional financial advisors you will need.

You are never too old to set another goal or to dream a new dream.
– C.S. Lewis, Irish writer and theologian

Chapter 1. What I am going to tell you.

"Tell them what you're going to tell them; tell them; then tell them what you told them." are the "Three Rules" for public speaking attributed to Winston Churchill. In any case, it takes three repetitions to penetrate my thick skull, so that is the model we are going to use here.

So, here is what I am going to tell you about:

- Making an income
- Managing your income
- Managing the risks to your income
- Insurance for risk management
- The fundamentals of investing
- Risk manage your investments too
- A secure but growing portfolio, and
- Pay less tax – it's your money

Making an income

Chapter 2 will provide advice on developing and growing the income from your labour and smarts. Once you have an income established, we can talk about making it stretch enough to provide you with your priorities. And the trouble you get into when you do not limit spending to those priorities: the evils of impulse spending, of putting wants ahead of needs. The result is DEBT, and it will mess up your life as well as your financial plan. Mind you, there is good debt as well as bad debt, so we will cover the difference.

Managing your income

Chapter 3 is an introduction to Management. Your monthly cash flow of revenue and expenses needs the same management processes as a Fortune 500 company. Management is a three step process of planning, taking action, and measuring results, done in a continuous loop where the findings from your results input to your planning, for the next month or the next business cycle. Planning is about projecting your revenue and expenses, then ensuring that the first exceeds the latter. Action may be what you do yourself or direct your team to undertake. But then you need to apply controls. That means measuring the results attained versus the goals projected, identifying the variance and determining the cause in order to take corrective action. You cannot manage what you do not measure.

Managing the risks to your income

In Chapter 4 we look at what can go wrong – short answer: anything and everything. A successful financial plan requires risk management. When, not if, your income is ended prematurely or unplanned costs hammer your income, what are you going to do about it? We can take precautions to reduce the chances of the risk happening, but we also need to make contingency plans to mitigate the damage should the risk occur. Whatever the source of your income - you could lose your job or lose your business, never take your income for granted. Network, improve your skills, know what is happening in your industry. If you should you get the short end of an office coup, it will not take you long to land on your feet. Learn to read the writing on the wall, and sell your business before the bottom falls out of your market. And look after your health – that can even get you lower insurance rates.

Insurance is risk management

Chapter 5 turns to risk management, in large part, by using insurance companies' financial products to replace income should certain risk events occur. We review the economics, and freakonomics, of the insurance industry – similar to lotteries, only with more serious bets. Premature death will have a dramatic effect on your income. You are not worth anything, but the net present value of all of your future income could well be worth a million or more. Life insurance should really be called "income" insurance because that is the asset it is insuring.

Whether or not you need to insure your income asset against the risk of premature death (one chance in 14 for a 40 year old before age 65) will depend on who is depending on that future income. If your priorities have included a family, then there may well be a need to replace at least some of your future income with capital to meet the on-going needs of the people you care about. If not, you may not need it where you are going.

A bigger risk to your income is a disability (one chance in five of 90 day plus disability) whether from illness or accident, where you are unable to work for some extended period. Likely, you will have already made commitments for at least some of your on-going income, obligations like a mortgage payment, not to mention eating. So plan your disability coverage as well as you plan for premature death. Either event could be the End of Work for you.

Insurance companies also sell critical illness (CI) insurance. This is called living insurance because it pays you should one of these CI risks occur (as high as one chance in three, or can exceed 50% for one of a couple). A CI event may not directly reduce your income, you could be diagnosed and still be able to work or practice, but the expense side of your plan can get hammered by drug costs, out-of-country medical, care-giving, et cetera. Your risk management could include a critical illness insurance policy, to provide the financial resources you need to successfully fight the big C, or you can self-insure this risk as you build up your own assets.

The fundamentals of investing

Chapter 6 introduces the final risk to your income, the End of Work. Will you sail off into the sunset on your own terms, or be put out to pasture prematurely, on minimal government income supports? Going out on your own terms will take up the balance of the book as we turn our attention to the money side. The majority of savers are not out to make a "killing" in the market, they simply want to protect wealth accumulation that can provide income when they choose to end work. The goal is long term, to achieve the wealth to provide you the independence to do as you wish with your remaining time and health – travel, volunteer, or continue in your profession because you still enjoy the work.

There are only two choices in investing. You can lend your money, or you can buy a piece of the business. Understanding the difference is the key to how fast you grow your wealth, with what risks. What are the right trade-offs between quickly and securely? There is no free lunch. You cannot have aggressive returns with conservative investing. The trick is to only be aggressive enough to reach your independence objective.

Risk manage your investments too

Chapter 7 returns to risk management. Chapter 5 was about managing the risks to your income in your earning years. Risk management for your investments will include balancing your portfolio with the right mix of aggressive and conservative investments, the benefits of diversification in reducing risk, and using dollar-cost-averaging to avoid the need to out-guess the market. There are even products that "insure" your capital just like you insured your income.

A secure but growing portfolio

Chapter 8 shows you a model portfolio with balance, diversification, and consistency to work towards your independence goal: would you believe the Canada Pension Plan? While you cannot (yet) buy shares in it, it can be a good model when looking for other balanced funds for your retirement portfolio.

Pay less tax – it's your money

You have established an income, you have insured it, and you are growing a risk-managed investment portfolio. Chapter 9 turns to the greatest risk to both your income and your investments – Canada Revenue Agency! Even before the glamorous ads with the sexy models entice you into a spiral of debt, the CRA (and its provincial and municipal counterparts) will have their hands in your pockets. There are ways, short of evasion that can send you to jail, to avoid at least some of the tax burden that is between you and becoming independently wealth. RRSPs are the best known tax planning tool, but now we have TFSAs as well; you need to know the differences and how to use each tool. Some insurance investments can provide tax sheltering like a TFSA. Then there are income-splitting opportunities, and the myriad of deductions and credits the government use to target specific interests and buy their votes. These change with one government to the next but be sure to use whatever is available.

What did I tell you?

Wrapping up in Chapter 10, I get to tell you what I told you. We will apply some of the lessons of financial planning so you can see how they apply in practice, to have a better idea of how to use them for yourself.

Chapter 2. The secret of success

Cash flow, cash flow, cash flow

An adage goes that the three secrets of (business) success are location, location and location. It might help a retail store or restaurant to be in a high traffic location, but the real secret of success in business or in the financial management of your life is cash flow, cash flow, and cash flow. The caveat is that net cash flow must be positive:

> *Annual income twenty pounds, annual expenditure nineteen and six, result happiness. Annual income twenty pounds, annual expenditure twenty pounds and six, result misery.*

Charles Dickens, my favourite economist, nailed the essence of financial planning. It is all about making money, while avoiding the road to ruin by spending more than you bring in. My contribution is to teach you how to manage the risks that can cut your income or add unplanned expenses.

What do you want to be when you grow up?

The first step before you even begin financial planning is to start making an income. So what do you want to be when you grow up? By the time you could walk and talk, parents and grandparents asked this question: cowboy, fireman, nurse, or a teacher? By your teens the choices might have become more sophisticated: Doctor, scientist, astronaut, lawyer, financial planner?

You should not take up a life course because of pressure from others. Your mother might want you to be a doctor but you want to be a rock star. Make your own choice. But then get realistic. The odds of a (financially successful) rock music career may be slim, so best get a trade as well – maybe medicine? You can still get weekend gigs to develop your music trade as well, so long as you have a means such as medicine or plumbing to make a living while you do.

Do not worry about making a wrong choice. Most of us will end up doing something other than what we trained for within five years of graduation. The majority of MBA students are engineers.

To the 17 or 18 year old, trying to decide what to do after graduating high school in the spring, my advice is more about what not to do. If you do not feel a drive toward a specific vocation, do not waste your time or your parents' money - it could be your inheritance someday. Make some money. Get a trade to make more money. Go to where the money is – Fort McMurray? Travel, see the world. You will grow up. You will know that you have when you realize maybe your parents aren't as dumb as you thought.

For the 35 or 40 year old feeling in a rut, better known as mid-life crisis, do not buy a sports car (unless you can pay cash) or look for a more exciting partner. But DO SOMETHING! The worst thing you can do is nothing. If you feel trapped in a boring job you no longer enjoy, but need to stay because of the pension, you should leave. Your mental health is worth more than financial security. ***"Bad things are not the worst things that can happen to us. NOTHING is the worst thing that can happen to us."*** (Richard Bach, my favourite philosopher). If you are not going to grab for the brass ring, get off the carousel.

Make some money

So whatever you want to be when you grow up, be something. As for the financial planning theme of this book, try to be something that you can make some money at.

Now you have grown up. You know yourself, at least better than at 18. You have a trade to make a living and you have a vocation that you enjoy. If you are extraordinarily lucky, it may be doing the same thing. But having a good trade that supports pursuit of your vocation is not a bad deal either.

Spending it

You have the first cash flow nailed, you have a pay cheque. The other half of "cash flow" is expenditures. You need to plan these as well as you planned for the income you work so hard for. Planning expenditures, actually consciously budgeting, is the first risk management tool to ensure your expenditures do not exceed your income. Resources are scarce and your pay cheque is not nearly as large you would like. That necessitates making choices, allocating scarce resources amongst competing priorities. The lease payment on the big truck that is such a great year-end deal may not make this cut. But if you do not subject that allocation to the test of your priorities, it may instead be your drive on the road to ruin. Keep needs and wants in their proper order: ***"You can't always get what you want, But if you try sometimes well you might find, you get what you need"*** (The Rolling Stones' Mick Jagger & Keith Richards, also pretty good philosophers).

Good financial planners, your mother or the Wealthy Barber, will all agree that your first priority is to pay yourself. No I am not talking about the truck (or sports car) lease. I am talking about saving. The first expenditure priority is taking a minimum of 10% of your net and socking it away long term where Einstein's eighth wonder of the world, compound interest, can work its magic. Ideally, you have it deducted from your pay cheque so it never goes into your bank account to tempt you.

Your second expenditure priority is debt. Many advisors would make this the first priority but I suggest it is more important to establish the saving/investing habit as early as possible. Chances are that by the time you are getting established you may have a variety of debts. In setting repayment priorities, understand the difference between bad debt and good debt. In a nutshell, good debt is expected to make a profit. Bad debt is blown out the window for fleeting pleasures. The big truck might compensate for feelings of inadequacy, but it is not going to make you money. The worst debt is financing consumption pleasures on high interest credit cards. You would be better off going to a loan shark – at least they will incentivize you to repay the debt! So get rid of your bad debt, starting with the highest cost debt.

Good debt is a student loan wisely invested for qualifications that will increase your earnings. It is reasonable to pay off good debt on a longer term schedule that matches the income returns it was invested for. Good debt can include leverage. Using a mortgage to buy your home (instead of paying rent), or a rental property that can provide a rental cash flow (hopefully positive). Having paid down your mortgage, good debt might include a HELOC (Home Equity Line Of Credit) at 4% used to invest in a portfolio targeting 8% - this is not without risk – see Chapter 4. After paying off bad debt, retire any good debt where the interest is not deductible. Then you might use your great credit for new good debt where the interest is tax deductible to make more money. This strategy can be used to make your "mortgage" tax deductible.

Only after paying yourself first, then managing debt, can you turn to your third priority, food and shelter. Yes, the necessities of life come ***after*** saving and debt payment. Finally, you may have some mad money left over for entertainment and other pleasures. You do need some of this too – all work makes Jack a dull boy. So even if you have to live in a smaller house or drive an older car, keep some scarce resources for some fun. Just pay cash as you go.

When you get that first real job, making $4000 a month, you soon realize that after government and other deductions, you really only make $3000. Add a deduction of $300 to pay yourself first, as well as at least as much, another $300 or so, on your debt retirement plan. You then realize you are really only making $2400 a month. Begin your budgeting from that point, not the $4000 you thought you were making.

Manage your expectations so that it will be easier to keep cash flow positive by only putting it out after it has come in. Now you have your cash flow established and allocated, we can turn to the day-to-day, year-to-year management of today's cash flow towards tomorrow's goal of financial independence.

Management is doing things right; leadership is doing the right things.

– Peter Drucker, Austrian-American writer and management consultant

Chapter3. How to Manage

Management in three words,

I have spent a lifetime in the study and practice of management, from Boy Scouts, military college, an air force officer, a Commerce degree, and the MBA program. Over a forty year career, I have managed operations in the public and private sector, run my own business and done a lot of management consulting. From all of that, let me teach you all you need to know about management in three words: Plan – Direct – Control. That really is all there is to it. Let me expand on what each task involves.

Where do you want to go?

The first step in planning is to pick a destination, specify a goal. By an accident of bureaucracy, I became a navigator, instead of a pilot like my Daddy. In a touch of serendipity, it has defined my approach to life. Being the captain of the ship does not appeal to me. I would rather sit in the back and figure things out. You can be the glamourous pilot, so long as you do what I say and go where I tell you.

Navigation has other lessons for managing or simply for living. Most people assume it is all very precise with careful measurement and precise calculations. But the manager or navigator rarely has complete information. The "Art" of navigation recognizes this in its lexicon with euphemisms like: dead-reckoning, most-probable-position, point-of-no-return. Half of the challenge in navigating or in managing or in financial planning is in making decisions with less than perfect information; some guesswork is usually necessary. Another euphemism for this process is using “repeated iterations”, otherwise known as trial and error. Keep trying till you get it right.

To guard against mistakes, or losing your way, always get two independent sources of information that corroborate your choice. Real airplane navigators have long been replaced with Global Positioning Systems, accurate to a few metres. But if the First Air pilot on his Arctic route had been corroborating the GPS information by observing the north star in his 10 o’clock position where it should be, instead of 12 o’clock where it was, he may have realized his mistake in setting the GPS and corrected it before he became a few hundred kilometres off track (and lost his job).

A variation of this navigation practice of corroborating sources of information is to always check your first answer. In our dependence on calculators, kids lose the mental arithmetic skills to check that 395 times 806 should be about 320,000 (round off to 4x8 and add four zeroes) so when the calculator read 31,837 instead of 318,370, I realized there was finger trouble on the keyboard and did it again.

We touched on choosing a destination in Chapter 2, in terms of deciding what you want to be when you grow up. You cannot start planning until you know where it is you want to go. You cannot solve a problem until you define what the problem is, you cannot manage a risk until you recognize it.

With that detail out of the way, you can start planning how you are going to get there (career choice) and what it is going to take (resources) and what can get in your way (Murphy's law). After choosing the destination or goal to be achieved, consider alternative methods and choose the best means available, collect and deploy the needed resources. The plan sets out the steps, the action plan, like the navigator's flight plan.

You cannot plan or manage without a destination or objective. But do not get hung up stressing about choosing the "right" destination. Circumstances or tastes may lead you to change the destination. The point for life or for financial planning is to have a destination or goal in mind, even if you may change it later. The latest Freakonomics tome, "Think Like a Freak", defines quitting and failing, not as disasters, but as learning experiences to help you get to the next destination. ***"Failure is simply the opportunity to begin again, this time more intelligently."*** (Henry Ford).

Executing the plan

The manager puts the plan into action by issuing directions to his minions - managers in large organizations do not actually do anything. The small business manager may simply change hats to become his own minion. This will often be the case in your financial planning where, after developing the plan, you will also need to execute the plan, to buy the insurance or make the investment.

Measuring is the essence of managing

The last task of the manager is the most often neglected: measuring the output being achieved by the execution of the plan to be sure it is in fact achieving the objective you set, on the schedule you expected. This may be tedious, but you cannot manage what you do not measure.

The navigator's job during the voyage or flight is to measure where the craft actually is by taking fixes of position (using independent, corroborating information). Differences from the calculated dead-reckoning planned position versus the actual position will be due to the environment being different – winds are never the same as forecast. The navigator then calculates the actual wind that put him where he is instead of where he planned to be, so that he can issue corrective action directions to the pilot to get back on track, to reach the destination as planned. Similarly, a manager's quarterly results may be less than projected due to economic pressures, competitor initiatives, higher input costs – or maybe he just made some mistakes. He can then analyze the causes of the variances from the planned results and amend the plan to achieve the year end goal. There is also the option to adjust the plan expectations. The original goal may have been unrealistic under the circumstances.

You need to do the same in your financial planning. You made allocations of your scarce resources to achieve certain outcomes. Regularly measure if you are achieving the desired results. If you find a target missed, then you can address "why". It may be that you blew the $300 mad money budget by the $200 great deal on the new outfit that was on sale at your favourite store. That's all right, you do not need to give yourself twenty lashes of recrimination. Simply recognize the problem and take corrective action – like forgoing planned concert tickets next month so that you pay off the high interest credit card in full by the due date.

Welcome to the real world

Plan, Direct and Control and your financial planning will be perfect, right? Sorry. The real world is messy. You may find yourself planning and directing and controlling in different spheres at the same time – job, family, finances. And the environment on which you based your assumptions will change like the wind, requiring new corrective actions. But however messy the real world becomes, keep the basic model in mind to keep you on track.

Trade-offs

Some might assume the manager's job is to maximize some goal such as profit. In fact it is a balance, to meet the profit target while avoiding going broke. Investing is the same, to make a return without losing the principal. Management is like juggling. The objective is not to throw one ball as high as possible; it is to keep several balls in the air at the same time.

You can classify each of your goals as a Need or Want, in choosing between priorities in your spending. You can also make trade-offs related to quantity and/or quality. I might "want" a twenty dollar bottle of wine but my "need" for a glass of red with my dinner may be 90% satisfied with a ten dollar bottle. I make a game out of trying to find a $10 wine that is comparable to a $20 bottle. Most people select their wines by grape variety or country/region. I like to shop by foreign exchange. When the rand is in the tank, South African wines can be a deal. With the euro down, many French wines became more affordable, and when the Canadian dollar was high, I was even drinking Californian.

Start with a wish list, narrow it down, but understand it will change frequently on this journey we call life. In the end the destination was not that important. It was the journey. Be sure to enjoy it.

The world doesn't care how many times you fall down, as long as it's one fewer than the number of times you get back up.
– Aaron Sorkin, American screenwriter

Chapter 4. Meet Mr. Murphy

What can go wrong?

So now you have established an income and set up a financial plan to invest in your future independence while retiring your present debt. Don't worry, be happy! Hold on a minute: ***"Whatever can go wrong, will go wrong. (at the worst possible time, in the worst possible way)"*** – *Murphy's Law*

What can end your work, and thereby interrupt or stop your income? You could lose your job in a merger, or get outsourced. But you have kept up your skills and networked so you will most likely be able to replace the lost income from the unplanned "end of work" fairly quickly.

What other life events could cut off your income? Premature death will certainly do that, but so long as there is no one depending on your income, like a spouse and children, this risk is not too serious from your point of view. Wherever you are going, you will not need an income. But if there are others dependent on your income, you will need to provide capital to replace the income that you no longer do.

Other risks can happen to your income. The risk of a disability, whether by illness or accident, is actually greater than premature death. Now you are not just worried about the spouse and kids, you need to worry about a roof over your own head and food in your fridge, along with the cost of retraining for a new field. You may have disability insurance as a benefit with the group insurance where you work. That's a start, but careful consideration is still needed in your financial planning to ensure your coverage is adequate, not just for your cost of living but also if you are carrying debts that must be paid whether you are working or not.

Other risks may not directly cut off your income but can impose major costs that have the same effect, driving your cash flow negative. The cost impact of a Critical Illness, even if you survive, can eat up your savings, drive you into debt, or ruin your retirement. The best motive for buying CI insurance can simply be to provide the resources that will greatly improve your odds of beating the critical illness.

Life risks compound as well. A 35 year old male non-smoker only has a 6% chance of dying before age 65. But the risk of a disability is 34% and of a critical illness is 26%. The combined risk of one of these events occurring by age 65 is 50%!

The biggest and most certain risk to your continuing income, and the lifestyle it supports, is retirement, the End of Work. When you "retire" should be your choice, but for every professional that keeps working to 75 because they love their vocation, there is a 55 year old who has been out-sourced and can't get a new job – age discrimination is real. Providing for income when work ends is the ultimate destination of financial planning, the independence of having choices. Keep the priority of choices for when you are 64 in mind and you may decide to postpone the new car. Maintain your allocation of resources to pay yourself first with your investments, applying dollar cost averaging with compound interest.

Your retirement income plan also needs to include meeting the risks of aging. You need to accumulate some wealth beyond what you need for your retirement cost of living, to provide resources to cope with third trimester risk events like critical illness or long term care.

Safety Management Systems

SMS provides a risk management framework for your financial planning. SMS was first developed for risk management in the nuclear industry, where the consequences of risk events can be somewhat catastrophic. Fifteen years ago, the Director General of Civil Aviation introduced SMS into civil aviation. While civil aviation by any measure or comparison is very, very safe, the essential difference is in being proactive about recognizing the risks in your operating environment, to explicitly take steps to minimize the risk of an occurrence, while pre-planning how to mitigate the impacts should the risk occur.

The first element is to make an explicit statement of policy, a commitment to your financial goals. This might be your commitment to put aside 10% of all net income towards your future. Another feature of an SMS policy is a requirement to have non-putative reporting. People are not going to report safety concerns or incidents if they are only going to be punished. In parallel, if guilt is your main motive for sticking to your financial planning, you won't. Failure is normal. When a tactic is failing, there is no need to beat your head against the same wall: quit, learn from mistakes, and find a new approach. ***Insanity is doing the same thing over and over again and expecting different results***. (Albert Einstein)

The second element is to have clearly defined roles and responsibilities for all team members. You do not do this on your own. You may be supported by your financial advisor, lawyer, accountant, mortgage broker, while your spouse and other family members will be stakeholders in your financial plan. Listen to them, communicate with them all, and be open to new ideas from all sources.

Third, you need to document your risk management performance just like you need to do for your financial performance, measuring the actual results achieved and comparing them to your planned objectives. Review results periodically, detect trends, identify root causes, then make a corrective action plan when performance falls short of targets, for both the short term (when you need to stop the bleeding) and for the long term to address root causes, to change how things are done to prevent recurrences. Then evaluate the effectiveness of the corrective actions, and be prepared to make further analysis and corrections.

The world is a messy place, so do not expect things to ever work out fully as planned. But keep the discipline of a system and you will stay close to track.

Go a step further. Instead of reacting as things happen, you proactively hypothesize risks what could happen. This is where thinking like Mr. Murphy can help. Pessimism is a tool to anticipate negative occurrences, and guard against them, even before they happen. You may decide to buy critical illness insurance, not out of guilt, but due to healthy pessimism.

Reviewing results regularly, including evaluation of the effectiveness of previous corrective actions, is the essence of a quality assurance system. Besides application in your financial planning, this can be usefully extended to other areas of your life, such as charting your career progress in your chosen vocation.

Emergencies – make a Will NOW!

The final element of your financial management plan is emergency planning. An SMS includes a requirement for formal emergency planning, about how all members of the team will respond, not if, but when an actual emergency occurs. Your financial plan deserves no less. That begins with having a Will, one that addresses how you or your partner will respond should something happen to one of you, and the role of your other financial team members. The Will planning process is not just about how your assets are to be dispersed. Its purposes include a living will for when you are not able to make decisions for yourself, as well as choosing an executor to look after your affairs and a guardian for your children.

Again, it is a lot easier to deal with a crisis when you have a plan set out in advance.

Not happy subjects perhaps, but they are reality. Dealing with them in advance will mitigate the impacts of a tragedy, for yourself and the people you care about. GET YOUR WILL DONE NOW.

When all else is lost, the future still remains. – Christian Nestell Bovee, American writer

Chapter 5. Insure your most valuable asset

We do not hesitate to insure our car or home. We see these things as assets which can be lost by accident or fire. If they were to be lost, it would be a huge burden to replace them. And liability claims in a car accident could truly ruin you. But these things are not your most valuable asset. Your most valuable asset is the net present value of the cash flow from your future earnings. You may be a successful early middle age professional at 35 making a nice $100,000 a year, doing better than most but not rich. Say after taxes and savings, about $50,000 is left to finance your lifestyle. What is your net income worth? Assuming you work till 65, $50,000 for 30 years is a net cash flow of $1,500,000. Discount it for inflation and the opportunity cost of money, gross it up for future raises and modest returns, and right now your income asset has a net value of better than $1.5 million. If you had other property worth $1.5 million, wouldn't you insure it?

This is also how you would value a business, not on how much its factory and equipment cost, but on how much money it is going to make with those inputs. You too are a factory, a money making machine. What is it worth to you? You hardly need to insure this asset if you are dead. But we tend to make commitments against our future income: we get married, have kids, buy a home. If you are dead, would you care about those depending on your income? If you love them, you might choose to risk manage the chance of premature death cutting off your future income that they are depending on. Insurance provides capital to replace the income that was provided by your labour. Insurance is not on you, it is on your future income asset.

Insurance economics

Before getting into different kinds of insurance, let's start by reviewing the economics of the insurance business. At the first level, it is about pooling risk. Say for any pool of a thousand homes, there is an expectation, based on statistical experience, of one burning down each year with a total loss of $250,000. Each of a 1000 home owners puts $250 a year into the pool. Whichever owner's house burns down is compensated for their loss with the $250,000 in that year's pool. The insurance company adds a margin for administrative costs, and profit, and the risk of higher than expected losses, a risk they may insure with other companies called re-insurers to further spread the risk in larger pools. The overall result may be an annual premium to insure your home of $500. Pooling risks is the actuarial basis of insurance.

However, you also need to appreciate the second foundation of insurance, behavioural economics. The psychology of economics is every bit as important as the mathematics.* Human behaviour is the foundation of the supply and demand curves: self-interested consumers buy more when the price goes down or sellers may put it on sale to move extra supply. Or self-interested sellers may hold back supply to keep the price up. Competition might then attract a new supplier who thinks they can make a buck offering a lower price. That's how it should work. But then the waters get muddied by marketers using techniques like branding. A distinctive brand on a generic product tries to convince a consumer that the branded product is worth more. Insurance companies are no different. They will all have special names to make their generic products sound different, or insert "features" to give an impression of more value. Marketers say that *"packaging is 90% of the product"*; an attractively presented product is more saleable, at a higher price.

The particular behaviour affecting insurance freakonomics is "risk aversion". This is the human tendency to buy more insurance as the risk of a loss gets greater or has greater impact.

Risk aversion behaviour creates a gap between the risk neutral pooled risk cost curve and what people are willing to pay for protection from the risk. This gap in the risk neutral versus the risk-averse curve is where insurance companies make their money. Your job is to realize that companies will try to capitalize on your fears to sell you more. You need to understand they are using this fear to move more product. You want to buy your insurance objectively, based on your needs, not on your fears.

The Undoing Project by Michael Lewis explains the development of behavioral economics, how an Israeli psychologist won the Nobel prize in economics.

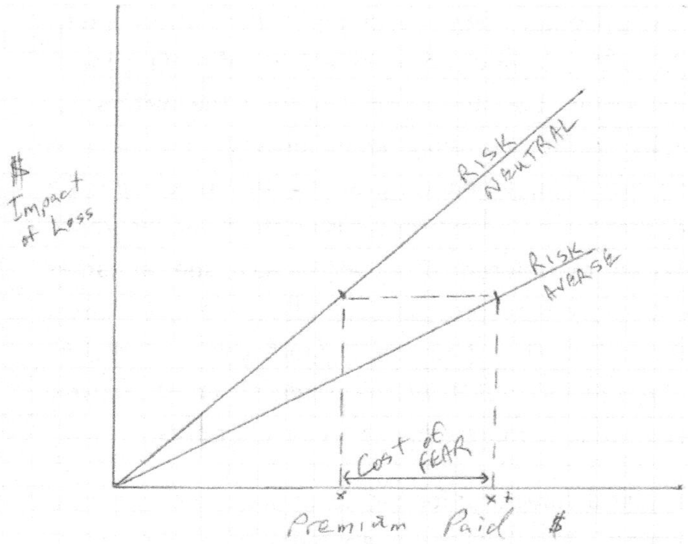

THE COST OF RISK AVERSION

The risk aversion curve of behavioural freakonomics also explains the lottery business. We all know that the chances of winning are remote, even stacked against us – lotteries make casino odds look generous. Nevertheless, if the reward is large enough, even though the possibility is miniscule, we are induced to risk-seeking behaviour and buy a ticket - the pay-off is so huge and the ticket cost so small. My freakonomics rationale is that I know I will only win the lottery if "God" wants me to. If God wants me to, all I need to do is buy one ticket. "I've done my part God, now make me rich!" Guess God wants me poor, but just in case He changes his mind, excuse me while I run out to get my ticket!

The third principle behind the insurance industry is insurability. Now hear this: ***insurance companies are not charities***. When you are betting that your premium is a fair price for the odds of you collecting, they are betting they will not have to pay. The result is that they will only offer insurance if you are a good risk. One of the most important things you can insure is your insurability. Even though a child may not have an income to insure, starting them off with a policy that provides some savings while also giving them guaranteed insurability options in the future can be worthwhile. For a young person just establishing their income, term insurance is so cheap at 25 or 30 that it can be a good investment just to protect your insurability for future protection needs. If you wait till you appreciate the need and importance of insurance, say at 45, you may have developed blood pressure, early diabetes or a myriad of other health concerns, or taken up a hazardous hobby, that will get you declined, or at best rated, by insurance companies.

You need to understand the rational economics of insurance, the pooling of risks, as well as the irrational marketing of insurance based on risk aversion and outright fear, and the risk of being able to plan for life's risks with insurance if you yourself are at risk of becoming not a good risk. Now you can look at buying insurance.

How much, for how long

You begin by defining the insurance you need. You will minimize the cost of insurance by buying the least amount needed for the shortest period of time. You can control the amount by self-insuring some of the risks. You choose to simply not insure some things, like foregoing collision insurance on your beater because a write-off would not be a huge loss that you couldn't afford to cover yourself. On the other hand you may choose to insure some of your critical illness risk, at least until your investment plan will build up enough wealth that you can self-insure it. Once you define a need, you can consider how long the need will last. If it is a temporary need, such as covering a mortgage liability, you can estimate the period of time that coverage is needed. Even if the mortgage has a 25 year amortization, your financial plan may provide for retiring it in 15 years. Why buy a plan with 25 year coverage if you only need fifteen? The insurance cost per thousand goes up as we age. The level premium in the 25 year contract factors that in, making the premium more costly.

Based on the ages of your children you might estimate how long extra income may be needed by the surviving spouse (or their guardians) for the "dependency" period, for the extra costs of child care. A marriage is like a business partnership where you may choose to take insurance on each other to provide for the continuation of the business or family.

You may choose to insure your investment plan for retirement income. Even if the children are gone, and the mortgage paid by 55, you might want to have the income the deceased spouse would have contributed to the partnership retirement plan had they lived to 65. Whether you include this need in your financial planning is an example of where you need to define the needs.

Finally, in defining needs, give yourself some flexibility. People tend to add to the mortgage for renovations, or moving to a bigger home. Some people do get behind the eight ball of debt. Home equity can help in debt management to get your life back on track. Another risk is that the children may not move out by 18. So keep some flexibility in your definition of your needs. Risk management means planning for unplanned needs as well.

In estimating the amount of risk for which you may need protection, there are three categories most planners consider. First is "Final Expenses". Besides planting you, this would include settling the estate, paying off debts, winding up a business, and any bequests. These needs tend to be more modest, say $50,000 to $100,000 but they will be permanent. You may need permanent insurance to cover Revenue Canada's share of your Will, a part of "estate planning". Financial planning is an on-going process. You need to successfully execute a financial plan for your independence, but you will also need a plan to protect your estate and legacy after you've gone.

Other insurance needs tend to be time-specific, such as for mortgage protection or to provide a surviving spouse extra resources to raise your children through the dependency period. The combined result is that overall insurance needs increase toward middle age, but may reduce through to retirement.

You may already be into your thirties with a couple of heirs. You already know it takes two incomes to support them. However, the dependency period does tend to wind down as they graduate post-secondary and maybe even move out. Then there are commitments like the mortgage, car leases, and lines of credit. Capital to pay these off reduces the cash flow income needed by the surviving spouse.

You apply the same analysis to your disability risk; how much of your income would need to be replaced, for how long? Another question is "how soon"? Employment Insurance gives you a short term disability benefit for seventeen weeks (why don't they say four months?). If you have a three to six month emergency fund squirreled away for short term needs, your cost of disability insurance would be less if you can self-insure the greater odds of the short term risk by opting for a longer waiting period for your personal disability insurance. Then there is the benefit period to choose. Many group and mortgage plans are limited to 24 months of benefits. Independent insurance plans will allow you options, such as five years or to age 65, at a higher premium of course. Again, you need to take responsibility for defining your need and for assessing your marginal benefit of any additional coverage for its additional cost.

If you have group coverage where you work, is it adequate? If not, what is the best way to make up the gap: self-insurance through a bigger emergency fund? Or buy a personal disability policy? If group coverage is a good portion of your disability risk management plan, how certain is it to continue? If your ambition is to start your own business in a few years, it may be a good idea to buy your own disability insurance now to be sure you have some coverage when you no longer have the group insurance benefits.

The rest of the insurance need calculation goes back to the risk management we talked about in the last chapter. First, identify what can go wrong, because it likely will sometime. Then see what actions you can take to reduce the risk probability. Give up sky-diving? Certainly quit smoking! Assess the impact of the risk occurring, how much of the risk you could cover with your own resources, and for any gap remaining, look into insurance coverage to pool your risk with others in the same boat.

Risk assessment can be emotional as well as rational. You may see the devastation to a colleague's family when she develops cancer and suddenly critical illness insurance may be more important to you. Do not discount emotional needs. They are real. Some guys really do need a big truck to compensate for other inadequacies. Financial planning should recognize your areas of weakness. Just keep your compensation actions as rational as possible – buy the big truck used.

What kind of insurance?

So you have made your best guess of the amount of insurance you need, and for how long, padded a bit for uncertainties. What kind should you buy? There are only two choices. Your vehicle can be leased or bought. Your house can be bought or rented. Same with insurance, you can rent it or buy it.

Term insurance is renting an amount of insurance coverage for a specified time. Permanent insurance is permanently in place, so long as the premiums are paid. It is possible that by the time you die you will have paid in more than the face value. On the other hand, if it is needed sooner, it is the 95 year olds, and more likely those who let their policies lapse or cashed them out early who will be making up the proceeds that your beneficiaries receive.

You may hear debates about which is *better*, for example, "buy term and invest the difference". One kind of insurance is no better than any other, there is only the *right* insurance for you: which product gives you the best value for your money in meeting your need, for the period that you have defined. Typically, the permanent needs are most cost-effectively covered by buying permanent insurance products. Defined period needs are more cost-effectively covered by *renting* term insurance.

For the insurance portion of your financial plan you have now defined a set of needs, in terms of amounts and the term of coverage you need to buy. It is time to go shopping.

Shopping for insurance

Let's compare to shopping for a car. You have defined your need as a four door sedan for the family and a panel van for your business. You visit a number of car dealers. They will all have different names for their sedans, and several models from compact to full size, all with a range of engine, transmission and trim options. So will the insurance companies. This is why you need to know how much of which size of sedan you actually need or length of lease you want on the van. Some of the options offered may sound of value to you. But like the better trim levels of a mid-sized sedan, there is a cost. Carefully evaluate if the marginal cost of a feature will give you more marginal utility, better value for your money, or is it just so much snake oil from the salesman?

I have a beef with insurance salesmen who sell "double indemnity", where the policy pays double the face value if you die accidentally. Everyone expects if they die prematurely, it will likely be in an accident, and the extra premium is not much. Reality check! Insurance companies are not charities. Double indemnity is only cheap because the odds are ten to one you will die from natural causes, even in your 30s, than from an accident. Secondly, remember you have defined the need, say for $500,000 of coverage. Buying a $250,000 policy with a double indemnity rider is not good risk protection. On the other hand, buying $500,000, then adding double indemnity is a waste of money. Buy a lottery ticket instead.

Term insurance is less open to product differentiation by the companies when they are trying to establish greater "value" in their brand names. The most common variants are ten year term or twenty year term. The shorter term costs less. It is covering less risk for younger ages when the cost per thousand is less than it is in the later years of the twenty year term. Insurance companies use T10 products as a bit of a loss leader to get clients signed up to their brand. However, if you have defined the need period as twenty years, say to pay off the mortgage and get the kids through college, then the higher premium T20 will be more cost effective over your defined term than renewing, at a much higher premium, after the first ten.

Like everything, there is an exception. The first need is to provide for the amount of coverage needed. You and your spouse might determine $500,000 coverage is the minimum need if one of you were lost now. But in your early thirties, in a new job, with two pre-schoolers and a new home, scarce resources are even scarcer. Even if the ideal plan says you should use $100,000 permanent and $400,000 term, it may be better at this point to use a ten year term for $500,000. That would cost $68.85/month for two thirty year old non-smokers, versus $231.48/month for the "better" combination. But build it into your plan to convert $100,000 of the term to permanent in five years.

There is one more thing you can do to reduce your cost of insurance: quit smoking. Even a social puff at a party in the last twelve months can classify you as a smoker, and the premiums are close to double. A smoker may be better off with a Term 10 and a financial plan to quit so that they could convert to a longer term at non-smoker rates in the future. This is managing a risk by reducing your risk factors. Insurance companies may not be charities but they are competitive businesses and will give you a better rate if you can give them a better risk.

A common need for term insurance is when buying a home and signing up for a mortgage. As an aside, the first insurance advice is to get a twenty percent down payment by hook or crook. You can only buy a home with 5% down by paying a huge up front insurance premium to Central Mortgage and Housing Corporation - and it only protects the lender. This cost is almost hidden when you are looking at whether you can afford the PIT payments. But in fact it eats up most of the 5% minimum down payment so your down payment "equity" is almost nil when you begin your mortgage payments.

Whatever financial institution you have applied to will also try to sell you "Mortgage" insurance, often giving the impression that you "have to" for the mortgage to be approved. This is called "tied-selling" and is a violation of regulations. It is also a bad deal. While you make the payments, the bank owns the insurance and makes itself the beneficiary. In some cases, an insurance contract is not even issued (very few bank officials are licensed to sell insurance). It is only "underwritten" when a claim is made and if there were any reason for denial of the original application such as a medical condition, no insurance payout is made. CBC's Market Place did an expose of this racket a few years ago; it is still on the net at: https://www.youtube.com/watch?v=qe61HVGIwUo. And the financial industry wonders why it has a bad reputation!

Insurance related to mortgages is another example of regulation not doing anything for you. All of the regulated requirements, from CMHC to title insurance and property insurance and traditional "mortgage" insurance only protect the lender. There is no regulation of any insurance requirement that protects you as the borrower!

More people are using mortgage brokers who deal with a variety of lenders and can advocate for you as the borrower. Benesure created Mortgage Protection Plan marketed through mortgage brokers. Coverage is underwritten by Manulife (who also bought Benesure a couple of years ago, it's an incestuous business.) Mortgage brokers are regulated by securities commissions and are not licensed to sell insurance. They just print the form, have you accept or waive, and fax it to Benesure. Your business relationship will be with Benesure, who will pay your broker a referral fee. MPP is an improvement over bank insurance in that you "own" it and can transfer the coverage between lenders if you want to renew your mortgage later with a different lender, but it has its own limitations in that the lender is still the beneficiary, and benefits are tied to and limited to the mortgage. Most financial planners today recommend covering a mortgage liability risk with independent term insurance that you own and designate the beneficiary, who can use the proceeds as most needed at that time.

There are other variations of term that an insurance broker, who also deals with multiple companies, can recommend to fully match your needs. Decreasing term products reduce to 50% of the face value over the first two thirds of the term, then level off at 50% for the rest of the term. This can better match a decreasing insurance amount need, as the kids get closer to independence and the mortgage gets paid down, while still giving adequate coverage for the rest of the term. Better matching the coverage to the need will reduce the cost. If a "mortgage" protection plan were maintained as it approached zero face value, one would be paying a lot for not much insurance.

There are three choices for insuring permanent needs. One is Term to 100, which always pays off but does not accumulate any investment value. The most common permanent insurance is Whole Life which accumulates an investment. The investment portion is controlled by the insurance company and it is invested very conservatively, partly because of regulations. Nevertheless, Whole Life can play a role in many financial plans at the conservative end of the portfolio.

The "new" form of permanent insurance is called Universal Life, again marketed by insurance companies under various brand names like Innovision or Genesis. Manulife recently updated its UL product line calling it "Manulife UL" – how innovative, calling something what it is! UL is the most flexible form of insurance offered today. It is effectively "buy term and invest the difference", but this strategy is combined into one contract, with legal and tax advantages. It gives you choices how you pay for the insurance (e.g. yearly renewable term or level cost of insurance) and whether you want the insurance to decline as the investment increases (level face value). You choose how you want the investments handled from fixed income to equities. The best feature is provided by CRA as the investment earnings are tax sheltered, like a TFSA. Yes, insurance should be part of your tax management strategy too.

In a complete financial plan, Universal Life can create your own insurance company for self-insuring risks in your last trimester, from critical illness to long term care to a pension supplement to legacy bequests, to paying off CRA to preserve your estate.

Where do I get it?

There are a wide range of choices when buying insurance. You can get life insurance from:

- A captive agent who represents one company
- There is the internet
- Your general insurance company (auto, home) will usually sell life insurance (even though they are regulated by the same body, they are not licensed the same as a life and health advisor)
- Affiliate groups like your professional association or alumni group have plans (and likely get a kick-back from the insurance company, but that may keep your dues down)
- The group plan where you work may offer optional add-ons (e.g. one time salary as a base plan but you can buy up to five times), or
- An independent licensed insurance broker will work with multiple well-known companies. A good financial advisor will help you work through what you need. You make the decision how much you need for how long, and then the advisor finds the alternative products to best provide the need that you have defined, without getting over-insured or not having enough, within your budget.

Doubt is not a pleasant condition, but certainty is an absurd one.

-- Voltaire, from The Undoing Project, by Michael Lewis

What are the risks in your financial life?

- ?
- ?
- ?

Chapter 6. Investment Choices

There are only two

You have committed 10% of your after tax earnings to paying yourself. You want to put it to work, to get a return to grow your wealth. There are only two things you can do with it. You can lend it to someone who will promise to pay you interest (you can be a bank!). This ranges from a "high interest savings account" for ½ of one per cent, a Guaranteed Investment Certificate paying 1 to 2%, up to a fund of corporate bonds, possibly including some real estate and infrastructure investments that might average 5%.

Your other choice is to buy a piece of the business. You can invest in your own business, on the side of your day job, or full time. A common on-the-side business is rental properties (you can be a slum landlord!). You can buy shares in a corporation, privately or on a stock market. You can buy units of a fund that owns a portfolio of stocks. Instead of a specified rate of interest, your investment return will be in dividends, the share of the profit paid out to shareholders, and in capital gains if you later sell the shares for more than you paid for them (at the risk of a capital loss if you *buy high and sell low*).

If you prefer to balance lending your money and buying the business, you can invest in a Balanced Fund which owns a mix of fixed income and equity assets. Depending on your risk preference, you can choose a fund with more or less of either lending or buying. A conservative balanced fund might have 70% fixed income assets while a more aggressive balanced fund could hold 70% in equities.

The trade-off is risk

What is the trade-off between lending your money versus buying a piece of the business? In short, it is the level of risk. In today's economy, with artificially low interest rates, you will need to take on some level of risk in order to achieve even conservative return targets. Returns from fixed income assets like savings accounts and GIC's won't even cover inflation and taxes. Relying only on fixed income investments, lending your money, you may not live long enough to save enough for an independent retirement.

Although a bond promises a fixed rate of interest, the guarantee is only as good as the issuer. Federal government bonds are more certain, they can always print more money, so may pay 2%. A provincial or municipal bond where they cannot print money, but can raise taxes, will pay 3 or 4%. A corporation which cannot do either may have to promise 5% on its bonds, but do you really anticipate General Electric or McDonalds may default on their bonds? But then General Motors did.

The borrower, the company that issues the bond, is expecting to invest it for higher returns and profits. So why not buy shares in the corporation and enjoy the higher returns yourself? Part of the answer is that the bondholders will get paid before you. So why not take the greater certainty of "fixed rate" investments?

One reason is that a $1000 bond is not always worth $1000. Say you owned a ten year bond paying 5% but decided to sell it after five years when current interest rates were 10%. You would only be able to sell it at a discount, say $950, because the purchaser would want to make the going rate of 10%, the bond interest 5% plus the gain to its maturity value of $1000. So even bond funds can have some volatility depending on prevailing interest rates, but not likely as much volatility as the stock market.

Conventional wisdom is that your choice of fixed income versus equity investments will depend on your risk profile, your tolerance for market ups and downs. If you are a risk-averse conservative investor you should stick to lending your money. If you are more risk-tolerant and aggressive, you should invest in ownership through equities where you will expect a greater return over the long term, even though short term returns may bounce between wonderful and losses.

The best mix for you, between stability or higher returns, will depend on your objective. The balance between lending your money in fixed income assets or buying a piece of the business through equities is not a function of your tolerance for risk, as advisors and regulators would suggest. It is a function of how much you need to make on your savings to reach your independence target. You can get by with a lower level of risk if you start soon enough, put enough away or set a more modest target. If you want more, are starting later, don't want to commit enough from current consumption, you will need to take on more risk. More risk means you may not meet your target. But not taking on the necessary level of risk will guarantee you do not make your target.

How much will you need?

The first step in choosing a long term average return target, and the associated amount of risk you may need to take, is to look at how much capital you will need for your *End of Work*. How much money are you going to need by age 65 to live *in the manner to which you have become accustomed?* Say you make $100,000 a year. That is pretty good by most standards.

You go to http://www.servicecanada.gc.ca/eng/services/pensions/payments-2015.shtml and project to receive $14,424 (average) up to $19,536 (maximum) from CPP & OAS.

Say you will have 25 years in the public sector with a defined benefit plan of 2% a year that will provide $50,000 in pension. Oh, you work in the private sector and have 30 years of a defined contribution plan? Better tone down that pension estimate to maybe $40,000 a year.

Your $100,000 today nets you about $60,000; you take off the costs of working: gas, parking, clothes, Timmy visits, but add into your budget for travel and other new pursuits, or longer Timmy's visits now you do not need to get back to work, and you may still need to net $60,000 for your desired life style. Even at a lower 39.4% Marginal Tax Rate instead of 43.4% MTR when working, and no longer paying pension deductions, you may still need about $90,000 gross to net that target independence income.

So if government and work pensions are expected to provide about $55,000 of income when you have retired, where are you going to get the other $25,000 to $35,000 of annual income? You plan to live to 90 so it needs to last 25 years. 4% is all the return you can expect at today's interest rates, even taking some modest risk. You will need somewhere in the order of $550,000 in your investments by age 65 to make that target income. If you have 20 years and $12,000 a year to invest, you will "only" need to realize 6.5% on average, a challenge in itself. But what if you can only afford to invest $500 a month? Then you would need to make better than 12% annually. To realize that return long term, you best have nerves of steel - and be very lucky.

You either need to start sooner and save more or you will need to use more risky investments. Maybe you will need to save $18,000 a year or retire at 70. What you can put in, by how long you have to your target retirement age, by what return you need to achieve, will define your investment objective for your financial independence. Start sooner, save more, and you can be more conservative – and certain of meeting your retirement targets. Start later and you may need to save more, be more aggressive, or both, and still risk retiring later if you fall short of your target.

You can look at the trade-offs for yourself at http://www.thecalculatorsite.com/finance/calculators/compoundinterestcalculator.php . Say you have accumulated $25,000 in your TFSA and you want to start your personal pension plan. How much will you need to invest at what rate to meet a goal of $550,000 for retirement? Say you are 35 so have 360 months. If you can only budget $200/month, but choose a conservative balanced portfolio with 30% equities that averages 6%, you will only reach $352,472. You will need more equities in your balanced portfolio, say 70%, hoping to achieve 8% that could reach $573,453, making your independence target by 65.

The higher rate means higher volatility. You may be reaching 65 in 2008 and be faced with a delay in your retirement date, due to the coincident market downturn. Or what if you are already 45 and only have 240 months to invest? Even if you double your deposits to $400/month, even taking more risk in a 70/30 balanced portfolio targeting 8% average return, you only reach $360,349 at 65. Even getting more aggressive, say 80% in equities trying to achieve 10% average return will only provide $489,481.

Start sooner, save more, or take more risk in your fixed income / equity balance. These are the trade-offs you will need to make in setting your investing goal. Your definition of the amount you will need within what time frame will determine the average rate of return you need. That will suggest the mix of equities and fixed income investment you will need, the amount of risk you will need to take on if you are to have a chance of meeting your target. You need to understand that the higher degree of risk in more equities means there is **less chance** of actually succeeding. But now you also know that if you stick to fixed income assets you would have **no chance** of reaching your independence goal.

You can also determine your independence target in reverse by calculating how much you will need to support your income target in retirement. How long will your money last? The following Table gives you a quickie guide. Pick the real interest return you expect to achieve with your investment funds after retirement, likely a more conservative level of say 4%. Then how years will it need to last? Life expectancy at 65 may be 85 for twenty years. But are you feeling lucky? Maybe you plan on living to 90 or even 95 which is not unreasonable. The figure in that box is the amount of annual income from each $100,000. Say your target is $36,000 a year, to supplement your government and employer pensions. Divide the number into $36,000 and times $100,000 for the amount of capital needed for your retirement objective. A realistic 4% return over thirty years of retirement will provide $5780 for each $100,000 in your retirement portfolio. You will then need $622,836 of capital (36,000/5780 x 100,000).

Take note that this projection is based on saving $200 to $400 a month for twenty to thirty years just to supplement your work and government pensions. What if you do not have a work pension? You will need to start your own pension plan, contributing both yours and your "employer's" shares. Go back through the same steps to calculate how much more you will need to produce another $40,000 a year from your "work" pension.

INCOME PROVIDED BY $100,000 CAPITAL

# Years to last	Income from each $100,000 @ Interest Return @4%	@6%	@8%	@10%
5	$22,460	$23,740	$25,050	$26,380
10	$12,330	$13,590	$14,900	$16,270
15	$8,990	$10,300	$11,680	$13,150
20	$7,360	$8,720	$10,190	$11,750
25	$6,400	$7,820	$9,370	$11,020
30	$5,780	$7,260	$8,880	$10,610

Or you can adjust your expectations. An optimistic 8% average return to last only twenty years will only need $353,288. You might plan to retire at 65, but are you willing to work till 70 if you need to? Or like the New Yorker cartoon, you can plan on taking an early death at 85.

Wither interest rates?

The portion of your investments to put into fixed income (lending) may depend on your view of the direction of interest rates. Current rates are artificially low with respect to economic expectations or norms of the past. Since 2008, governments have been keeping interest rates low to fight the Great Recession. Nothing screws up the economy more than government policies – but that is a different book. The result is that the most secure fixed rate investments no longer even cover inflation, never mind grow in real terms. But if you expect some rationality to eventually be restored in interest rates, you might opt to keep a larger portion in the "lending" type of investments.

Financial planning, even *for those with better things to do,* is not a totally set and forget formula. Periodically, you must "re-balance" your mix of lending and buying. Say today your target for independence requires averaging 8% net after fees for thirty years (with 2% inflation) and that needs a higher risk 70% in equities, because of today's low risk government bonds at only 2%. But what if sanity is restored in government monetary policy and secure bonds again pay 4%? You may be able to reduce your more volatile equity "buying" proportion to 60%, thereby lowering the overall volatility in expected returns. On the other hand (forgive me, I used to be an economist), you may only be achieving 7% and need to re-balance to 80% equities, striving to realize 9%, to make up the shortfall and have a decent chance of reaching your goal. The alternative to keep your 60/40 balance target is to start saving more each month. You may also want to rebalance as you get closer to retirement age, at least moving the funds you will need for the first few years into fixed rate "lending" assets.

The eighth wonder of the world

Even more important than the rate of return you need to average is the question of how long you are going to have for the magic of compound interest, Einstein's eighth wonder of the world, to reach your target? Money that earns interest on its previously earned interest will grow exponentially, that means the curve measuring total value increases, at an increasing rate. That is good if you are investing, bad if you are in debt to a loan shark or a credit card company.

You can estimate the impact of compound interest with the rule of 72. Divide 72 by the interest rate and the answer is the number of years that it will take the money to double in value. Or divide 72 by the years you have available to double your money and the answer is the rate of return you will need to achieve. If you choose only lending your money in fixed rate investments, with a variety of government and corporate bonds with an average return of 4%, it will take 18 years for your money to double. If you invest a $50,000 windfall at 29, for retirement at 65, it will double twice to $200,000. But if you invested in stocks and realized a 12% average return, you would double your money every six years. In 36 years, it would double six times: $100,000 after six years grows to $200,000 in twelve that becomes $400,000 after 18 years and $800,000 in 24 years, doubling to $1,600,000 after 30 years (you might decide to retire early if you reached that!) and a whopping $3,200,000 over 36 years. The difference in your retirement fund would be $3,000,000. With that kind of difference, why would anyone invest in fixed income investments?

Partly because a 12% return over the long term would be about the same chance as winning a lottery. But the one word answer is 2008. After the dot com bubble, and the 9-11 crisis, investors had been doing very well with equities. Then a bunch of greedy bankers* caused the 2008 financial crisis and many, many people saw their retirement portfolio lose up to half of its value. Maybe they should have stuck with bonds. Many panicked and locked in their loss. Others rode it out and recovered most of the loss over the next year or two. That is how the economic cycle works.

> *Michael Lewis explains how it went in the Blind Side. Pretty scary stuff that even I had trouble following. Greed has no limits.

Best of both worlds

Are there any other choices? A current popular trend is “value” stocks. These are large established companies operating globally with long histories of profits – returns they use to pay dividends to their shareholders, often at a growing rate. A steady stream of dividends can be a better cash flow than interest on bonds at the same rate because of their preferred tax treatment. People have long chosen equities for their capital gains. Dividend paying stocks are a happy medium, sort of like a balanced fund in one stock certificate with dividends providing income; any capital gain is a bonus.

Say you establish $800,000 (in current dollars) as a solid retirement goal, or at least your measure of financial independence. Then you only need your $50,000 to double four times instead of six. Divide 72 by the number of years we are targeting to double our money and you have the interest rate goal you need to achieve. To double four times in 36 years (starting at 29) only needs 9 years each. You can double your money in 9 years with 8% average rate of return. So you can trade off some of the risk of trying to achieve an unrealistic real return of 12% for 35 years for a higher probability that you might average 8% with a lower level of risk. You might arrange that by choosing a more balanced "balanced fund" with say a 50/50 mix of fixed income assets and equities. Even then, think about committing a little more every month to your investment deposits and a more realistic long run return of 6% may be enough to reach your target for independence. Start sooner, and markets do better, and you might even reach your independence goal sooner!

We all want to get the best possible return while taking the least possible risk, both in terms of the volatility of returns and especially, of any risk of principal losses. Regulators require advisors to complete your risk profile, whether you are a conservative or aggressive investor, in selecting investment products to recommend. Answering the risk tolerance questions honestly may result in the advisor only recommending fixed income investments that will take you 100 years to reach your independence target. You will most likely need a mix of conservative and aggressive investments. You have to make the decision based on your needs. The rate of return required to reach your objective may require taking a higher degree of risk. You then need to appreciate the possible impact from a more aggressive strategy, such as not retiring when you had planned to in 2008, but working a couple of more years while your portfolio recovered.

To lever or not to lever

One of my themes has been that taking some risks may be necessary. Advisors and investors may counsel using "good" debt, expected to make a profit, to increase the size of your investment portfolio. Using debt to invest is called "leverage" and that entails a certain degree of risk in itself. Say you have a $500,000 house with a $200,000 mortgage; there is a $300,000 asset that is not doing much (beyond an average 1% a year in market appreciation). Freeing up some of that money to invest would be getting double duty from it. So you could take out a $200,000 HELOC (Home equity line of credit) and buy a balanced fund of dividend-paying equities. Yes, that is leverage, and it can be dangerous, but it can be a reasonably managed risk if your investment choice is modest. Beware of the advisor appealing to your greed promising fantastic returns for little risk. Throwing it all into a hot mining stock that will make you rich by next year is not managing the risk associated with leverage – go to Vegas instead.

Most businesses use a mix of equity and debt in their capital structure. Shares in a company with a 50/50 equity/debt balance sheet might be considered a reasonable business risk. But personally for you as your own small business, I would keep even good debt under one third of your total assets. When it comes to borrowing for investment, i.e. leverage, my rule of thumb is to have any debt covered twice over by assets.

It would be better if you didn't need to use leverage at all, if you had started soon enough and saved enough and have more modest expectations. Leverage is an appealing idea for investors to magnify their gains (and advisors to increase their commissions) but leverage can just as easily magnify your losses. Nevertheless, using some leverage may help to meet your objective. If you have an $800,000 objective to meet your independence goal and only twenty years to do it, is it better to put your available funds into aggressive equities to try to achieve an unlikely 12% return? Or use some leverage to give you a better chance of making your goal, with a balanced portfolio projecting a more modest 8% long term return? That is one of the choices you will have to make. Like everything in life, using leverage is a trade-off.

Improving your returns – guaranteed!

There is one guaranteed way to improve your investment returns and that is to pay less in fees for financial services. Managing your money does cost money and we should not mind a fair price for service and expertise rendered. The difficulty is in knowing the price. Regulators require some disclosure about fees now; requirements became more stringent in July 2016, but even then you may not know the questions to ask. Commercials in 2017 have been featuring incredulous clients reviewing their year-end statements and finally realizing how much they have actually been paying in financial management fees.

Warren Buffett shared similar advice in his most recent letter, which you can find at
http://www.berkshirehathaway.com/letters/2016ltr.pdf
(pp 21-25) "The bottom line: When trillions of dollars are managed by Wall Streeters charging high fees, it will usually be the managers who reap outsized profits, not the clients."

Prices can be a shell game. One example is the grocery store chain that "sells" you a free membership (that lets them track your habits and target promotions to you). Then they mark special prices on sale items "for member's only". Of course you only select the item because the member only price is attractive. But you still feel good at check-out when you swipe the member card and see the 10 to 20% discount taken. And then they take your Air Miles card, and you use your credit card for more points – your groceries feel almost free! But do you have a clue what you really paid for the frozen pizza or pint of raspberries? The people who push financial products are no better than their grocery store counterparts.

One of my peeves with money-side advisors is that they tell you they are charging a fee for service, not a commission. But if the fee is a percentage, generally one to two per cent depending on the size of the portfolio, that is applied whether their management makes you money or not, then what is the difference from paying a commission on the dollars you invest?

You see the 1% management fee on your annual investment report (that the regulators require her to give you). And the new disclosure rules mean you also see the $5000 fee that one per cent of your $500,000 portfolio paid her. What did she actually do for you for that payment? Even at a comparable legal or accounting fee of $250 an hour, that is 20 hours of work. If you only met with her for an hour, what did she do for the other 19 hours? Do you allocate some of the 1000 hours she spent on continuing education and analyzing markets for your account, as well as amongst her other hundred clients? But wait a minute, professionals justify the $250 an hour fee for all those indirect costs. Can you find a financial planner who will "only" charge a flat $250 an hour? Even if you buy ten hours of her expertise, you will have saved half the fees compared to the other "fees only" advisor at 1%. Retired friends bragged about their wonderful advisor who had given them tickets in his box for a great game. They had likely paid for those "gift" tickets several times over.

You may think your financial planner takes the high road of being a fees-only advisor, so she must be working for you and not the commission paying supplier. But besides the fees that you pay, what is she getting on the other side of the transaction, from the purveyors of the investment funds where she has allocated your assets? Many pay trailer commissions that are hidden in the Management Expense Ratios (MERs). So besides getting one per cent from you, she might be getting one per cent from Investors, Clarington, Franklin Templeton, et cetera.

Whether it is an airline charging for a checked bag or a grocery store charging a nickel for a plastic bag, don't expect your financial planner to be far behind, nickel and diming you with every little administrative or transaction service fee.

The sneaky one is "deferred sales charges". Investing for the long term, it should not be an issue, but it is good to appreciate what you are really spending on fees to manage your money. When a fund is sold with a DSC, a commission is being paid to the advisor or their firm. It is re-covered by the investment firm in the MER charged annually before you even see the rate of return on your investments. A good test of the honesty of your advisor is when they recommend moving money from a fund you have held several years, so the DSC no longer applies, into a new fund where a new DSC liability will kick in.

So read your contract with your advisor carefully, and watch for details like service fees to withdraw money or move your account. You are the customer, it is up to you to demand transparency, and then evaluate whether you are getting value for your money in what you are paying to have it managed.

You may have read how robots will take over one in three jobs over the next few years. This applied to financial advisers as well. You now have a choice of using a "Robo-Advisor" at quite reasonable fees. The trouble with robots like all digital equipment especially computers, is that they just do what you tell them. But once you have invested in your financial literacy (by reading this book), you may not need a human advisor. You will know enough to give your robo-advisor directions that will achieve your goals.

In understanding what you are paying for money management, besides your adviser, you pay for the managers of the funds that you have in your portfolio. When it comes to high MER fees on actively managed funds, the net margin achieved rarely exceeds the comparable index over the long term. So some investors go with index funds at minimal fees hoping to at least chase the index. There is a wide selection of Exchange Traded Funds (ETFs) with only nominal fees.

Investors today have the choice of robo-advisors pursuing their directions with balanced ETFs. That route will cost far less that the all too common approach today of paying a financial adviser and paying an active fund manager. The trade-off is taking more responsibility for yourself.

There is one way to avoid MERs all together and that is to buy stocks directly, with modest trading fees. But we have already established that you do not have the interest or time to pick your own stocks. So just buy one that already owns a diversified portfolio, a conglomerate. The most famous is a share of Berkshire Hathaway where you get Warren Buffett as your portfolio manager. A Canadian example is Prem Watsa's Fairfax Financial Holdings, with a thirty year track record.

Be wary buying advice

While good advisors are invaluable in keeping you on track, and in finding the best track for you to reach your destination, an advisor who may not have your best interest at heart can do a great deal of damage to your financial health – think Bernie Madoff! Here are some tips to avoid an unethical advisor preying on your ignorance and trust. Remember that every dollar you save in fees comes out of his pocket.

A good test of an honest advisor is how hard it is to get transparency information out of them. If they seem to bend over backwards to be sure you know how much you are paying them, and still justify their value-proposition, you have a good one. Don't get suckered by one that seems to be costing less. The industry all has similar structures; chances are the "cheaper" advisor is not being as transparent.

Watch for an advisor who pushes you to take out an investment loan (that demon "leverage") so that you can buy more of what he is selling. The pitch goes: "You can be the bank. Borrow at 4% and invest at 8%" (or even more when he only tells you about the fund's growth in the past year of 20+% and doesn't show you the ten year 2% average). There is no free lunch. You only get 8% by taking double the risk compared to a 4% return on investment. The investment loan pitch says the investment is the collateral, but somehow when it gets set up the bank wants your house pledged as well. In 2008 when the market dropped 50%, the investment no longer covered the debt and people lost their homes. Conservative advisors will just tell you not to borrow at all to invest. My advice is to only borrow what you have to in order to perhaps reach your independence goal, while recognizing the risk that you may not, due to using leverage.

Beware the fortune teller. Nobody knows what the market will do, especially over the short term. Be wary of the advisor who assures you the price of oil (gold, potash) is going up 50% within the next year.

Complicated products such as "principal protected notes" usually include big up front commissions for advisors. If you do not understand the product, don't buy it – or that advisor's advice.

Finally watch out for an advisor who is always recommending trading, to move out of one fund into another with better recent returns. He may just be looking for a new commission and the new fund will reset the DSC.

Investing wrap

Every investment choice boils down to lending your money, or buying a piece of the business. That sounds simple, but all computer programming is just zeros and ones, yet there is an endless array of new "apps". Investing also has an endless array of financial products jazzed up to get you rich quick, or at least make a big return with hardly any risk. I attended a seminar where a reputable international banker was explaining how they reduce risk (volatility) by two thirds through sophisticated diversification. Yet when I asked what their balance was he couldn't tell me. I agree that diversification is important but I do not buy that it can reduce risk by that much, the world is just too correlated, especially today.

If you really want to know more about choosing some of these products for yourself, then you are a DIY investor, not someone with better things to do. Buy Don's book, sign up for Motley Fool newsletters, and all the other advice and web sites. But if you do not care to make that effort, because you have better things to do with your time, then you will need to seek professional advice on the best products to choose to meet the goals that you set. Just be careful in selecting and following advice. But that is why you have read this book, to understand how it works and what to watch out for.

By now you have learned some of the language so that you can talk to advisors and understand what they are saying. And if you cannot understand what they are saying about a product recommendation, whether it is lending your money or buying a piece of a business, and where the expected return versus risk trade-offs are, then do not buy it. And look for an advisor who can make herself understood.

And when you feel more confident, try a robo-adviser and move your funds into ETFs matched to your objectives.

Life is not a matter of holding good cards, but of playing a poor hand well.
-- Robert Louis Stevenson, Scottish writer

7. *Insuring your investments*

Manage the risk

Once you have established an income, your financial plan included insuring your income asset. You applied self-insurance by networking and continuing education to make you attractive to employers, and you bought life and disability insurance to protect your family and yourself. Once you are establishing a portfolio of investments that will generate your future income, you need to insure that asset as well.

Self-insurance

The first self-insurance risk management involves balancing between fixed income and equities, between lending your money and buying a piece of the business. Secondly, you self-insure your portfolio and reduce risk by diversifying between sectors and geographies. The third self-insurance is in being consistent in your investing, using dollar-cost-averaging.

Let's talk about risk, the bane of growing your financial independence – what can go wrong will go wrong. Most of us think of risk as losing our bet, or losing our capital, the risk of loss. But financial planners talk about risk as "volatility", the chance that returns may vary. In market downturns, you may even see negative returns implying a loss of principal, at least temporarily. "Guaranteed" investments, such as lending your money to a bank through buying their GICs, have a set rate of return. Remember that a fixed rate guarantee is only as good as the guarantor. And if you do need to sell your bond on the market before its maturity, its value on the market can vary by the change in the interest rate level. Your $1000 ten year 5% bond may only be worth $950 at year five if interest rates have gone up - there can be some volatility risk in fixed asset investments as well.

Buying a piece of the business through equities does not guarantee your return. The trade-off is that over time you expect to make a higher return on average, even though your returns may be more "volatile" year to year. Volatility is what a planner or banker has in mind when they ask about your tolerance for risk. Someone who gets upset by crashes like 2008 should lean to fixed income investments. If you are sophisticated enough to see the crash of 2008 as a "buying opportunity", like Prime Minister Harper (dumb politics but good economics), then you could put the larger share of your investments into equities. A balanced approach uses some of both so that when stocks are down in the normal course of the business cycle, the effect on your overall portfolio should be "balanced", hopefully staying positive but at least declining in total much less than the market. Too many DIYs invest by emotion. They buy high and sell low. They react to the latest trend or fad to get rich quick, and buy the latest hot stock near its peak price, just before it crashes and then they sell it low in panic.

Determining the split between less volatile "lending your money" investments versus more volatile but higher return "buying a piece of the business" investments depends on your retirement income objective that we talked about in chapter 6. A self-insured portfolio would likely have at least 30% in fixed assets and likely closer to 50%, especially as you approach retirement. And if you do not start soon enough or commit enough you may have to take more volatility in a higher ratio of equities.

Risk or hazard?

Just as we distinguish between risk as a total loss versus risk as the normal volatility of markets, it is useful to understand the difference between a risk and a hazard. A risk can be measured as the probability of an occurrence, based on statistical data. Actuaries at insurance companies use mortality statistics to calculate the probability of a pool of forty year olds buying term 10 insurance contracts getting to collect, and set premiums accordingly. A hazard, however, can be a random event with no apparent cause. To look at the distinction in insurance terms, you can reduce the risk/probability of premature death by lifestyle choices: get healthy, eat right, exercise, give up sky-diving, and QUIT SMOKING. Your insurance application will rate you accordingly.

Getting struck by lightning is more of a hazard, there wasn't much you could do about cutting the odds. That is why the cost of accident insurance does not depend on your health profile. And it is cheap because the probability of a forty year old getting killed by lightning, versus a heart attack, is much lower.

The short term behaviour of stock markets is a hazard, in the sense it is often irrational, responding to emotional investors. It cannot be predicted, it can only be ridden out. *"I can calculate the motion of the heavenly bodies, but not the madness of people"* said Sir Isaac Newton, after losing a fortune in the South Sea Bubble of 1720. If Isaac Newton could not figure out stock markets what hope do you have?

Instead, focus on under-lying demands, or to put it in Safety Management System terms, the root causes for expected performance over the longer term. An example is that wherever the economy is going one month to the next, people have to eat, brush their teeth, buy gas and pay bills. Companies like McDonalds, Proctor & Gamble, Exxon and the big banks are going to do business, make profits and pay dividends, even if their stock price slips in a down market. Over the long term, they are going to grow in value as they make ever greater profits.

Based on their stock prices, they have a "capitalization" of what the market as a whole thinks they are worth and big companies are classed as large cap stocks. They are not likely to go broke, so there is no more risk of losing your capital than there is of a sovereign government defaulting on its bonds (except Greece did). So invest in companies of intrinsic value and forget volatility. Buy equities of stalwart companies that have been around longer than you and forget about the risk of losing your capital, even if your net worth does vary on paper year to year with market swings – your annual cash flow from your dividends will not be affected.

If you really want to get in on the next big thing, and make a windfall to brag about at cocktail parties, take a small part of your money and gamble. It is not investing as in paying yourself first. It is a consumption activity, like buying lottery tickets. If you do make a killing, treat it as a random windfall. Allocate it by reverse psychology: give 20% to future gambling and invest the rest in non-risky ways.

In short, my sacrilegious advice is to eliminate the consideration of risk in your investing. Or more accurately, consider risk at the strategic level in choosing the fixed income versus equities balance, the risk you need to take to have a shot at your independence goal. Then select a professional advisor to find you good investments, and you will have already dealt with the risk factor. Or use a robo-advisor to select some balanced, diversified ETFs. Do not then respond to day-to-day variations in valuations, or even to 2008 "crashes". Ride out your choices without regard to market volatility. Only make rebalancing choices based on fundamentals, not on other people's emotions.

Diversify

After selecting your mix between fixed income and equity assets, you need to diversify. That means investing in sectors that are not correlated, which do not simply move up and down together affected by similar forces. Economic activities and the companies pursuing them can be classified in sectors. Five sectors are commodities, financials, consumables, energy, and utilities. You balance your investments amongst sectors with non-correlated volatilities, so that, for example, when financials go down, consumables go up.

Diversification is also based on geography. Canada generally did pretty well in the 2008 crisis (didn't lose as much as others). But the TSX does not provide a diversified portfolio. The relatively small Canadian market is dominated by Financials (34.7%), Energy (25.2%) and Materials (12.9%). So not only is diversification limited across sectors but their trend behaviour tends to be correlated, they all go up and down in sync so there is little compensation between them. There are 14,000 businesses in the MSCI World index. Only 20.1% are Financials, 9.6% are Energy companies and 5.8% are in the materials sector. If you stuck to a Canadian TSX ETF for your diversification, you would be missing out on Consumer Discretionary at 12.3%, Information Technologies at 11.7%, Industrials at 11.3%, Healthcare at 11.2% and Consumer Staples at 10.1%.

U.S. equities are a much larger pond that is more widely diversified across sectors. We may be motivated by patriotism to invest in Canadian small cap funds, but as much or more of your portfolio should be in U.S. equities. Then there is the rest of the world to consider. Europe may not have fared as well as North America in the 2008 crash but it is still a very large and diverse market. There are large economies in the BRIC countries (Brazil, Russia, Indonesia & China), and "emerging markets" like South Africa. There is a trade-off between higher growth rates and more volatility over the short/medium term, but these markets still deserve some consideration in your portfolio.

Be consistent

After balance and diversification, your next risk management strategy is consistency. This is called dollar-cost-averaging. That simply means that if you save the same 10% every month, you do not need to worry about catching the market. When the market goes down, your same monthly dollars buy more shares. When the market recovers, as it always does, you end up owning more units of your investment. Let me show you. If you had $1200 to invest, which investment from the chart would you buy?

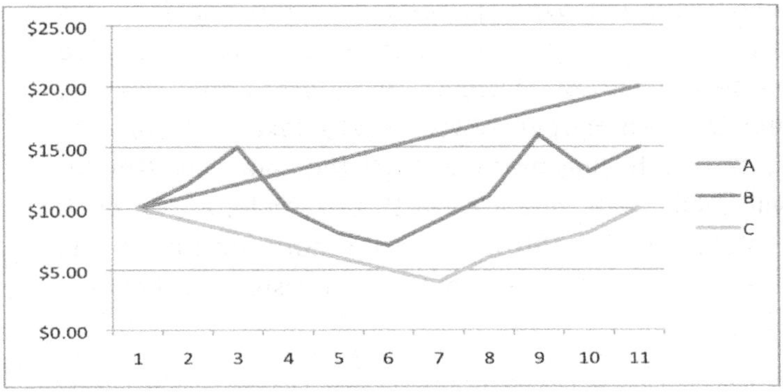

With investment A, your investment grows from $1200 to $2400. (Doubling in 12 years imputes a 6% annual return, according to Einstein.) Investment B would have grown to $1800 and Investment C would have recovered to the original $1200 investment, a rate of return of zero.

But what if you invested $100 each period instead of the $1200 at the beginning? Now which investment would give you the best return?

Believe it or not, investment C would be the winner giving you a portfolio value of $1741.27 while steady investment A and more volatile B would both end up at about $1595. When investing regularly, dollar cost averaging works in your favour throughout the normal cycles of up and down in the stock market.

Dollar cost averaging is really an investment concept where you systematically invest a fixed amount of money every period to buy investments that have a fluctuating price. Look at the math of investment C as a mutual fund with a starting price of $10 per unit. When prices drop as the market swings downward, investors often get concerned because the value of their portfolio drops. However, with dollar cost averaging, you and Stephen Harper systematically take advantage of price drops by buying more units of the same investment. You will finally be buying low! In this example, as the price drops in the first 7 months, more and more units are being bought each month for the same $100 invested, as shown in this table.

Dollar Cost Averaging

Month	Amount Invested	price per unit	Units bought	Cumulative units	Cumulative Value
1	$ 100.00	$ 10.00	10.00	10.00	$ 100.00
2	$ 100.00	$ 9.00	11.11	21.11	$ 190.00
3	$ 100.00	$ 8.00	12.50	33.61	$ 268.89
4	$ 100.00	$ 7.00	14.29	47.90	$ 335.28
5	$ 100.00	$ 6.00	16.67	64.56	$ 387.38
6	$ 100.00	$ 5.00	20.00	84.56	$ 422.82
7	$ 100.00	$ 4.00	25.00	109.56	$ 438.25
8	$ 100.00	$ 6.00	16.67	126.23	$ 757.38
9	$ 100.00	$ 7.00	14.29	140.52	$ 983.61
10	$ 100.00	$ 8.00	12.50	153.02	$ 1,224.13
11	$ 100.00	$ 9.00	11.11	164.13	$ 1,477.14
12	$ 100.00	$ 10.00	10.00	174.13	$ 1,741.27

At the end of twelve periods, with the market recovering in price to the original $10 per unit, your $1200 of investment is now worth $1741.27. In fact when the market crashed in 2008, if you had kept buying equities through 2008 & 2009 your portfolio would be worth far more by 2010 than it was at the start of 2008 even though the "index" had only recovered to its pre-crash level. I do admit that watching this investment failing to match your contributions over the first eight months would be a challenge when it does not exceed your contributions till the ninth month. That is why I keep saying choose wisely, then do not look at it.

Self-insuring your investments through risk management is just an approach of balance between bonds and stocks, diversifying between sectors and geographies and dollar-cost-averaging consistency in your investing. Its objective is first to preserve the capital by avoiding gambling. You invest in governments and corporations who you trust to keep their contracts and pay the promised interest. You invest in companies with intrinsic value, long records of earning profits and paying dividends. Or just use an advisor to find you a balanced fund with those components. And perhaps you allocate 5 to 10% to "emerging markets". On the other end, you may keep some investment in very conservative products like permanent insurance. A complete investment portfolio will include both conservative and aggressive investments.

Computers just make it worse

Looking at the long term change in the equity index, I have noticed a scary trend. It seems that during the past twenty years the index has become more volatile, with a major dip associated with the Asian currency crisis of September 1998, the March 2000 dot.com crash and the September 2001 terrorist attacks, then with the September 2008 financial crisis.

My theory is that this is due to too much information feeding the behavioural anxieties of investors. In this environment of computerized trading and stop-loss orders, overall indices have become more volatile. But that just makes dollar cost-averaging consistency that much more important. And you will note that despite the increased volatility, the trend line is steadily upwards, which is why you invest in equities, buying a piece of the business for that growth factor.

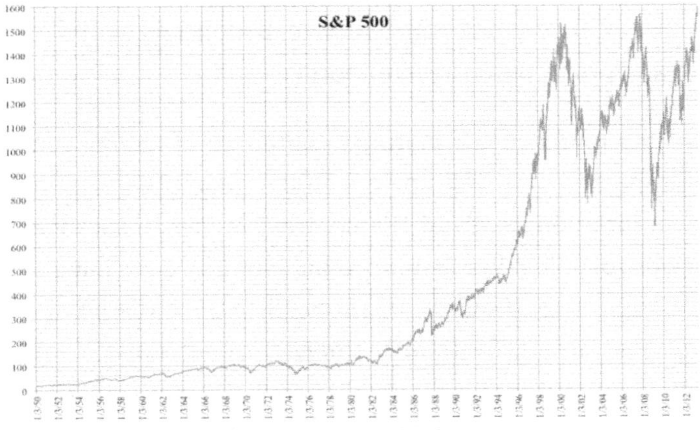

Insure your investments

Just as for personal risk management protection, self-insurance of your portfolio by balanced asset allocation, diversification and consistency will only take you so far. Then you buy insurance to pool your risks. Many investors do not even know that one can insure equity investments. All big financial companies sell investment mutual funds. Insurance companies also offer "Segregated Funds", often the exact same mutual fund but with an insurance "wrapper". The term simply means that these funds are separate, or "segregated" from, the insurance company's own funds that support its obligations under its insurance contracts.

To make a fund an insurance product to be sold by an insurance company, the company insures the capital with guarantees on the principal, at maturity or on the owner's death. This also makes a segregated fund an insurance contract, with all the advantages provided by law to insurance: tax free proceeds, direct to beneficiary without probate, and protection from creditors.

Typically, seg funds offer a maturity guarantee of 75% of the original deposit (some sell up to a 100% guarantee) and a 100% guarantee on death of the contract holder. Insurance on your portfolio, just like insurance on your life, does have a cost. The typical seg fund premium is 15 to 25 basis points added to the same MER (Management Expense Ratio) that the underlying mutual fund would charge. If you were risk managing a stock purchase, you might buy an option to protect your downside. A seg fund is the same idea, paying a (modest) price for protection; along with the insurance feature advantages, it can be good value.

The best feature of seg funds is that most of these contracts include a "reset" feature. Say the original $100,000 investment had a 75% guarantee. If the market crashed tomorrow, your worst down side would be $75,000. But after the investment grew to $133,000, you could have the guarantee reset to $100,000 (75% of the then value) thus locking in the guarantee to insure your full $100,000 original investment. The second guarantee is typically 100% on death before maturity. The major benefit here, if you are investing funds to grow your "legacy" account for heirs and favourite causes (but still want to own it in case you ever need it while still alive), is that 100% of the fund's value is paid directly to your beneficiaries – TAX FREE as insurance proceeds. There is no deemed and taxable capital gain as there would be on a mutual fund. That tax benefit is worth a few basis points right there!

Most planners suggest shifting more of your portfolio to fixed income investments as you age, to protect your pension income and heirs from the volatility of markets. Seg funds allow you to continue participating in equity investments, at least for the portion of your funds with a time horizon of at least five years to ride out any one economic cycle.

Buy term and invest the difference

You can insure your investments as well as your life with a Universal Life permanent insurance policy. When mutual funds were a hot fad in the 1970s and 1980s, many salesmen recommended buying only term insurance so that you could invest the rest of your savings money into "high return" mutual funds. People who were still doing this in 2008, without insuring their portfolios, "lost" half or more of their retirement savings. A great number of people then sold low (after buying high) to save what they had left. And locked into low rate fixed income investments with no chance of ever recovering their volatility losses.

A Universal Life insurance contract is basically buying term and investing the difference. A UL contract provides the tax preferred treatment of life insurance, direct payment to beneficiaries without probate, but it also provides the tax sheltering of investment returns like a TFSA. Growing your wealth with a UL investment can allow you to be your own insurance company for a critical illness, long term care, or even to supplement your retirement pension income. And when you do pass on, it provides your executor liquidity to protect your life's work assets by paying off Revenue Canada's take.

Insurance companies are getting more creative at packaging UL products that better help you to minimize insurance costs while providing a full range of investment funds, with simpler administration and lower MERs.

Insure your retirement

Before you sail off into the sunset are there any more risks to consider in your financial planning?

Yes, you may live too long. Running out of money is another risk your financial plan needs to consider. The rule of thumb in the financial planning community is that you can take 4% a year from your portfolio and you should not run out of money before you die.

But without a defined benefit pension plan, you may have some challenges even with that conservative withdrawal rate. Along with a modest defined contribution pension plan, most of your savings will likely be in registered plans. Come 71, the government forces you to change your registered savings plan to a registered income fund. Mandatory RRIF withdrawals start at 5.28% at age 71 but go up to 11.92% by age 90. The stipulated minimum withdrawals rules were just lowered to reflect longer life expectancies in the 2015 budget. So how can you manage this risk to your on-going income in your third trimester? You could cut back your withdrawal rate to 3.5% or even 3%; the C.D. Howe Institute recommends the mandatory RRIF withdrawal rate be reduced to 2.68% to make your money last.

There is one other strategy. You can take your financial independence money and *buy* a defined benefit pension plan. Insurance companies sell them as annuities. There are many options: joint life, fractional payments for the later life, and guarantee periods, so that all or most of your money comes back to your estate if you croak too soon. You pay for certainty by pooling the risk. Sure it has a price. You just have to be optimistic it will be paid by those poor life style losers who are going to croak first, while you enjoy a long retirement guaranteed to never run out of money. The insurance company is applying the same economics explained in chapter 4 when they sell you an annuity, diversifying over a pool of lives.

Financial planning is using your income earning years to accumulate the wealth that will provide your income in your retirement years, to give you the independence to do as you want. Pay yourself first, set a target, figure out the return required to make it, choose a balance of investment products to provide that return, put Einstein to work as early as you can. Manage your risks with diversification and dollar-cost-averaging. Use insured investment products. That's all there is to it.

If the highest aim of a captain were to preserve his ship, he would keep it in port forever.
--Thomas Aquinas, Italian priest, philosopher and theologian

8. A Model Portfolio

Balanced, diversified, consistent

So what does a balanced and diversified portfolio look like? Would you believe the Canada Pension Plan? A financial advisor selling you any investment fund is required to provide you a "Funds Fact Sheet" that includes the fund's investment policy. Here is the CPP's: *"The cornerstone of a successful investment strategy is effective risk management. We are required to adhere to investment policies, standards and procedures that a prudent person would exercise in dealing with the property of others."* One could readily adapt that statement in their own financial planning SMS policy, substituting "my property" for the property of others. That is the essence of what the last chapter was all about.

The CPP used to get lousy returns. Governments used it as easy money, where they could borrow your money at ridiculously low interest rates instead of raising your taxes directly. It was a big portion of government debt and another shell in the public finance shell game of how politicians use our money to bribe us with promises while getting their gold plated jobs with platinum defined benefit pension plans while the rest of us struggle to use what we have left to make the most of a defined contribution pension plan, if we even have that. But I digress. **"SHELL GAME – understanding public finance"** is my next book. Let me tell you how to fix you first, then we can fix government. For now, I just wanted to give you an example of the risk management tactics I have been advocating.

The former CPP investment portfolio in government bonds was not dissimilar to the average saver, approaching retirement, with their savings wasting away in GICs, slowly losing capital after taxes and inflation were considered.

Government realized twenty years ago that the CPP was going bankrupt long before most of us alive today would get to collect benefits. Typical of politicians, they created the CPP Investment Board to manage the CPP funds. Now if CPP went broke, it wouldn't be their fault! As a professional and independent management organization, the CPPIB have done very well with our money. Most of us need a similar plan, to reduce our low interest fixed income investments and get into balanced, blue chip, large cap, dividend paying equities, diversified across sectors and around the world.

The CPPIB is governed and managed independently from the CPP, operating at arm's length from government and with a singular objective: **to maximize the returns without undue risk of loss.** Working with the right advisor (even a robo-adviser), you can be your own CPPIB.

Let's see how they are doing with our money, looking over the last Annual Report for the year ended March 31st, 2016. Start with the principle of balance. The CPPIB asset mix is down the middle with 52.3% in equities and 47.7% in fixed income investments. The objective of balance is to provide respectable and steady returns for the long term, but the other side of that coin means returns are not stellar either. The rate of return (after costs) was only 3.4% for the year ended March 31, 2016. But the TSX/S&P500 index was down9.7% for the same period. That is what balance will do for you. Markets go up & down; balanced funds go up and down less. In 2008/9 when the TSX was down 35.5%, the CPPIB was only down 18.6%, half of the market's downturn volatility was dampened by having the balance of fixed income assets. Incorporating "Balance" in your portfolio means being content at 10%, when others are bragging about a 20% return, so that you can be consoled when they are "losing" half their fortune and you are only temporarily down a fraction of that.

In choosing your asset allocation, I had recommended against gambling, but maybe just a little is OK. Even CPPIB has 6.3% of its assets in equities in emerging markets. Yes, they may be more volatile, but they are expected to give higher returns. Just like you might use a permanent insurance policy at the conservative end of your portfolio, six or seven cents on the dollar at the high volatility end is not too much gambling. I told you earlier to ignore risk in choosing your allocation of assets. Perhaps I should have said "balance your risks". 10% in high volatility emerging market equities can be offset by 10 % in conservative investments like insurance, but keep the other 80% of your retirement savings in balanced funds, similar to the 50/50 mix found in the CPP.

Diversity is applied by the CPPIB geographically by only having 31% invested in Canadian assets while 69% is invested globally. The proportions are even more dramatic in its equities portfolio where only 5.4% of its assets are invested in Canadian equities while 40.6% are in foreign developed markets. So if you are feeling unpatriotic about putting some of your RRSP in a U.S. large cap fund, don't feel guilty. Money is global. If you want to feel patriotic, go to a Jets game and yell "TRUE NORTH" during the anthem. And the CPPIB has its equity investments well diversified across economic sectors as well.

CPPIB's fixed asset portfolio is 19.4% of assets in bonds and money market securities but has 13.2% in real estate, and its infrastructure investments have reached 7.6% of its assets; toll highways and bridges are great cash flow generators.

With all working Canadians' pay cheques being docked 4.95%, matched by their employers, every month, the CPPIB is receiving a steady cash flow to be invested though all market cycles, using the power of dollar-cost-averaging effectively. You need to be sure your financial planning is working with a similar 10% of your cash flow.

If you feel inclined, buy a rental property. It is also easy to leverage through a mortgage. Just know what you are doing as it is an active investment. You will need to maintain it, oversee your tenant and collect your rent. For those with better things to do, you might consider a real estate fund for a similar 10% of your portfolio.

At $298.1 billion (December 31, 2016), the CPPIB is managing one of the world's ten largest pension plans. Headquartered in Toronto, it has offices in London, Hong Kong, New York and Brazil. With its track record, you may think that would be a great financial product for your retirement savings plan. There is only one problem, the CPP has not (yet) been opened up to allow you to make additional investments. Last year the Provinces (who have to pay most income support programs, like welfare for the destitute) pushed for the CPP scope to be expanded. The Harper feds resisted but Justin made a deal to raise premiums, phasing in so the mandatory employer matching contributions wouldn't be too much of a drag on the economy. With the CPPIB's performance I worked out that they could substantially increase benefits without increasing premiums by making it a defined contribution plan with individual accounts – a debate for another day perhaps.

Similar portfolios

In the meantime, what are your options for an affordable, well performing yet conservative, balanced personal "pension" investment? You could select balanced investment funds that mirror the CPPIB, or find a fund close to it if you want to avoid even that decision. The Saskatchewan Pension Plan is an example. It is a defined contribution pension plan (unlike CPP's defined benefit advantage). It allows contributions up to $2500 a year that are RRSP eligible if you have the room (& most of us do). While you may have never heard of the SPP, it is the 27th largest such plan in Canada at some $300 million. The economy of scale provides professional active management at a fee of only 1% compared to the average MER of investment funds of 2.53%. The return since inception has been a very reasonable 8.13%.

Unlike your RRSP, it is a locked-in pension plan. That means you cannot withdraw for buying a house, upgrading education or just to spend it. On the other hand, that may be an advantage for at least a portion of your investment savings.

If you think you may need access to your money, simply work with an advisor to pick a mix of seg funds with monthly contributions that provide balance and diversity: A Canadian small cap fund, a U.S. large cap income fund, a global equities fund and an emerging markets fund, for the equity 50%, and a corporate bond fund for fixed assets. On the annual review, you can discuss macro-economic trends and perhaps rebalance how much is going into each choice. Like if Trump makes you nervous, move ore into fixed income for the next four years.

And CPP is not the only big game in town. Manulife, as one example, has over $300 billion of assets under management.

A Dianne Maley column in the Globe and Mail (Saturday, November 8, 2014) featured two actively managed balanced funds for the core of your portfolio; the more senior fund, with a 60/40 balance of equities and bonds, had an 8.5%

average return over twenty years, through all the recent turmoil, and after a very reasonable MER of 0.96%. Invest $50,000 at age 35 and your money will double four times as you approach 65 for an $800,000 retirement fund objective. So if "you don't have the time or inclination for do-it-yourself investment" you can still "seek the comfort of knowing someone is at the helm", at an affordable cost.

This example may be out if date by the time you read the book, but it is offered as what you pay a financial advisor by the hour for, to help you construct your own CPP.

Construct your own

I will close this portfolio building chapter with one more example for the conservative end of your savings: start your own insurance company. We already talked about budgeting for an adequate income in retirement to support your chosen life style. We also talked about major hits on your income that can screw up your retirement: a critical illness, long term care, or other unforeseen crises, or just to top-up your retirement income when your returns fall a little short, to cover that special trip you have been planning. But isn't starting your own insurance company expensive? Not really. That is because the insurance companies will be happy to sell you one, in the form of a Universal Life tax-sheltered investment contract. You can use the CPP balanced model in selecting your Universal Life investment funds.

True happiness is ... to enjoy the present, without anxious dependence upon the future. --
Seneca, Roman philosopher

9. *Tax Planning*

Whose money is it?

It's your money, not Revenue Canada's. Politicians have an insatiable appetite for your money. They need it to buy your votes and $20 orange juice. Provincial and municipal politicians and empire building bureaucrats are no better than Revenue Canada. And it keeps getting more and more complex, mostly because politicians do not want us to see when they are picking our pockets. Public finance is no better than a shell game, but that is the subject of another book.

There was once a day, I am told, when people willingly paid their taxes as their contribution for the greater good. But that was back in the middle ages of "tithing". A tithe was 10%, not a bad price to pay for a reasonable bundle of public services. But today when the three levels of government extract 50% of our gross, and tax freedom day is later and later in June each year, we are not as likely to feel happy about paying taxes of whatever form. After food and rent and enjoying life somewhat, it gets ever more difficult to find the 10% needed to pay ourselves first towards our eventual financial independence. Just as important as avoiding frivolous spending, or high interest credit card debt, or excessive fees for financial advice, you need to pay attention to ensure you are not paying any more tax than you absolutely have to.

Evasion versus avoidance

We do need to pay the legal taxes. (Keep in mind that the legal system is totally uncorrelated to a justice system.) There is an important difference between tax evasion and tax avoidance. The first can lead to a jail term. The second is legal and keeps more cash for you to invest in your future. Tax lawyers and accountants, not much different from financial advisors, will milk you for fees to advise you how to avoid paying some tax. While you will need these professionals to keep you out of jail, you can be more effective if you understand the principles. We talked earlier about financial literacy, just knowing enough to choose the right strategy, even when you use a financial advisor for tactical choices in selecting the actual investment products. This chapter is about the basic principles of tax literacy so you can make more effective use of the tax professionals, without paying excessive fees.

A long time ago I took a full year, six credit hour course in income tax. I hated the subject and got the bare C+ needed to pass. But I did learn two things. One was that if our situation was ever too complicated for a T1 Short (the old paper tax returns), then get a professional, because it is a full time job to stay on top of all that stuff. Today we might say if you need more than Quick Tax Basic, get professional help.

The four D's

The second thing I learned was the four D's of tax planning. The first D is DEFER. That is simply deferring paying taxes as long as you (legally) can. Most people are happy to get a tax refund in April. They should not be. A refund simply means that you have given the government more of your money than legally required. And they do not pay you interest on your free loan to them. The principle of deferment is to organize your affairs to pay as little as possible until they ask you for it by an assessment. You may even get away with fibbing a little, such as on the TD1 form you file with your employer for calculating your deductions. It can be truthful to say you have a spouse or children, even if you expect them to make enough money that you may not be able to claim them as deductions next April. You do not have to tell your employer that as they would then have to deduct more tax. And did I mention you do not submit your tax return (or at least post-date your cheque) till the 30th of April?

Different sources of income can be deferred better than others. The best is business income where you can incorporate and select a year end early in the calendar year. Say you want to use the government fiscal year; maybe a lot of your clients are public sector so it is helpful to be on the same fiscal year. That means money earned in the year ending March 31st was three quarters earned in the previous calendar year. Plus you have six months for a corporate return which gets you to August 31st instead of April 30th for personal income tax returns (even if tax owing by a corporation must be paid within 90 days, or in the case of a holding company, it is only 60 days – keeping all this straight is why you use a tax professional). Personal and corporate tax rates, and personal situations, will determine the right amount of income to take into your hands personally for your own tax reporting; that is another reason you use a tax professional, to figure out the optimum split. Take some money you made on a deal closed in April year one. The income is reported by your corporation at year end, March 31st year two, and pays corporate taxes due from that income on June 30th year two. Say a certain amount of that income from the April year one deal was declared to you March 31st year two. It is income you receive personally in year two that you do not need to report on your personal return that is only due April 30th of year three. Income received as salary in April year one would have been deducted from your pay cheque in April year one. Structuring your affairs to have the income taken through a corporation, then paid to you for declaring on your next personal return, has deferred the tax for two years. If it was $10,000, with a marginal tax rate of 40%, what could you have done with that $4000 in your jeans instead of in the government's consolidated revenue fund for those two years?

The best known tax deferment is by having investments in RRSPs. You can defer the tax and thereby invest more pre-tax dollars and the earnings are also sheltered. But an RRSP only defers the payment of the taxes due. The only avoidance is if the withdrawals are made when you are in a lower tax bracket, such as after retiring.

Deduct

The second D of tax literacy is DEDUCT. On your personal salary income, your TD1 form, you deduct your personal exemption. Be sure to deduct any others you can legitimately claim (like dependent spouse and children). On self-employed or corporate income, the scope is broader on what you can justify as expenses that are legitimate to deduct because they relate to making that income. Revenue Canada has all kinds of rules to limit your ability to deduct; staying within these rules is another example of how a creative accountant can pay for herself. Having a small home based business on the side that generates some of your income from self-employment allows you to deduct some of your household and transportation and other costs that you may well have incurred anyway. The principle is that you have to link the deduction to the income. Fees related to investments, for example, are quite legitimate deductions from that income. Any deductions you do not take is money left on the government table, not kept on yours.

Divide

The third D is DIVIDE. The idea behind dividing income is to get an overall lower tax rate. The main example is between spouses. The U.S. tax system allows family income to be taxed together. The Conservative government got on the tax-splitting band wagon by allowing pension splitting between seniors. They promised income-splitting in support of families where a higher income spouse could split her income with the stay-at-home-spouse. The family would still have the same $100,000 income, it would just be taxed as two incomes of $50,000, where the rate of tax would be lower, and hence the amount of tax paid is less. But that didn't seem "fair" to the new Liberal government so never made it to the tax books. Whether that is sound policy or not I will leave to the Shell Game book. An already available tax division strategy is a private corporation where the husband and wife are 50/50 shareholders. Some income from the corporation can be taken as salaries but this may be limited to what would be a reasonable role for the less active spouse. However, shareholders can take equal dividends.

Now if we just had a flat tax at the same rate for individuals, families and corporations, on all sources of income, wouldn't life be a lot simpler! But think of all the accountants, lawyers and financial advice book writers who would be out of a job.

Dividend

Some tax experts stop at three D's but I think the fourth, DIVIDEND, is worth including. It serves as an example of taking advantage of legal preferential tax treatment. The idea is that dividends have already been taxed at the corporate level before the cash flows out to shareholders as dividends, so some allowance should be made in its treatment to reduce the double taxing of the same income (just making dividends from Canadian corporations tax-free would be the simple way to do the same thing but bureaucrats never do anything the simple way). The tax treatment of dividends can get quite complicated. Your job in being tax literate is to ensure your tax professional helps you take advantage of structuring some income as dividends to reduce your net taxes payable.

Capital gains also receive preferential tax treatment so I include them in this D. The theory is there is higher risk in making this income so it should not be taxed as heavily as more secure income like interest and salaries. It was rumoured that the Liberals were going to take away some of this benefit in the last budget but they backed off (for now). The flip side of the Dividend tax literacy D is to take as little as possible of your income in salary and interest as these attract the highest rate of tax.

Tax shelters

In recent years, the government has given us another legal means of tax avoidance. A Tax Free Savings Account allows money already taxed to then earn income without further tax on the investment income. This makes it an excellent vehicle for non-tax-preferred income, like interest on fixed income assets. Besides tax relief, a TFSA's features are very flexible for your financial planning. And don't forget that a Universal Life investment can also grow tax-sheltered like a TFSA.

Integration

So long as you are keeping the four Ds in mind you may see opportunities to integrate them as well. Taking income as a capital gain, because of the preferential rate treatment, is also a means of deferring tax because income is not realized until the asset is disposed. You may be paying half rate tax on a stock sale gain where most of the gain was made years ago.

Save yourself sitting through a whole year course in income tax, believe me, you have better things to do. Practice the four Ds in your approach, and find a creative professional to help you apply them. Avoid as much tax as you can for as long as you can, but do not fall over the tax evasion cliff.

Getting money out

In retirement you are going to live on your company pension and your RRSP, as well as CPP and OAS. All of these are taxable. A couple keeping taxable income to about $60,000 each (by income splitting), will hopefully be paying less tax than what was deferred when putting these funds into tax-deductible investments, say 34% versus the 44% that was deferred on contributions, and all that time, the funds were growing without tax. You will also avoid the claw-back of OAS if your individual incomes are kept under the $73,756 threshold (2016) as the combined effect of the claw back on income higher could work out to a marginal rate higher than your RRSP deferral.

The ultimate tax shelter is insurance. Remember starting your own insurance company as the conservative part of your portfolio in chapter 7? Any of this money can be used tax-free because it will not be income. You will not withdraw it either so that it can continue to grow. How do you do that?

You borrow it from your friendly neighbourhood bank. But what bank is going to lend you money in retirement, when income is less? Any bank will because you have perfect guaranteed collateral – your universal life insurance policy! (They know you are going to die.)

Say you had established a $100,000 Universal Life contract at 45 that had accumulated a $60,000 personal insurance fund. Say you make use of it (through borrowing) with $20,000 for extra travel from 60 to 70; $20,000 for out-of-country medical and drug costs to beat a critical illness at 75; and $20,000 to pay for better quality care from 80 to your eventual passing at 90. Yes those loans from the bank will have accumulated interest – did I mention you never need to make a payment on those loans? But it is unlikely that the total of principal and interest will exceed the $97,000 value the fund will have grown to by age 90.

So why did the bank wait so patiently for its money? First, repayment was guaranteed by being first beneficiary on the insurance policy. But the bank's second motivation for its generosity was because insurance benefits are tax free: the bank just got all that accumulated interest income as a non-taxable insurance payment instead of interest income on which it would have had to pay tax!

And last but not least, remember the original $100,000 insurance face value? It is still there even after the bank loan and interest are paid off, to look after Revenue Canada's final grab.

The biggest hit Revenue Canada makes on Canadians is when they die. Any registered investments are deemed to be cashed out, any assets that have generated capital gains, like the family cottage, are deemed to have been sold at fair market value on the date of death. Your total estate may only be some $200,000 when you finally pass at 90, after a healthy and well financed 30 years of financial freedom. But that $200,000 of net income the day you die will attract the highest marginal rate of tax, call it 50% with other fees and costs to wind things up. That $100,000 of insurance, after the bank gets paid back, will pay your final tax bill so that your estate is preserved for what you want it to do - all tax free. Your own insurance company can look after the final phase of your financial planning, your estate planning. For spouses, where these assets can transfer tax free, insurance costs can be lowered by basing them on a joint last to die policy since that is when the tax liability will kick in.

Don't delay

Better yet, in retirement, rather than defer till the big tax hit on death, take out registered money sooner, even though you will pay tax on it. Remember the rationale of the RRSP is to defer tax when you are at the highest bracket with the expectation that when you withdraw it you will be taxed at a lower rate. Not only will you have had all that registered money working for you all those years, you will actually be avoiding some tax, not just deferring it.

Besides the four D's of tax planning, avoiding tax all together is even better. An example: in my province of Manitoba, you pay 50.4% marginal tax rate (federal & provincial combined) on taxable income over $202,800 (2017). A successful business person or professional could well make $220,000. Putting $10,000 in her RRSP in 2017 would defer $5020 of taxes. In 2018 she retires and takes $75,000 in taxable income for a reasonable life style. Her MTR drops to 37.9%, and it stays at that MTR up to $91,831. It is time to switch gears from the DEFER mindset. Take the $10,000 back out. There will be 20% withholding tax (on $5000 to $15,000 withdrawals - so do it December 31, 2017). Your tax return April 30, 2018 will be paying $1790 more tax to make up the $3790 total tax due. However, you will have actually avoided paying $700 in taxes ($5020-$3790=$1230). That is a lot of numbers to show every bit helps. And $1230 really saved would buy a nice week in Mexico.

Similarly, use whatever room you have within your retirement MTR to de-register money as quickly as possible, and re-invest it. It the example, you could withdraw another $16,830 at the 37.9% marginal rate. You could put that after tax money into tax preferred equity investments with capital gains and dividends taxed at lower net rates. Or in a tax shelter like TFSAs so that the fixed income highest marginal rate returns are sheltered.

Too many people stay in the tax-deferment mind set in retirement, and take only the minimum RIFF withdrawals as they become mandatory. With registered investments, you should not think of it as your retirement fund of $500,000. Only $250,000 is yours, the other $250,000 is CRA's that the government has only "loaned" to you. Treat it as a debt to pay off as quickly as possible. Set up a schedule of withdrawals up to your MTR upper limit to deregister the whole RRSP and with returns, in a dozen years or so, the $500,000 will actually belong to you. In this phase, you can use insurance investments like segregated funds and universal life policies to continue growing, as well as protecting, the converted funds.

Life is a blank canvas, and you need to throw all the paint on it you can.

-- Danny Kaye, American actor and singer

10. What did I tell you?

A financial plan – for those with better things to do

You need to do financial planning to look after yourself, and others you love. You are responsible enough to give it some attention, but would prefer to dispense with the requirement as painlessly as possible. Here is the Plan for you.

- Make some money. Hopefully at something you enjoy doing, but if not, something that will finance what you really want to do.
- The secret of success is cash flow, cash flow, cash flow. Keep it positive!
- Money needs to be managed. That means PLANNING what you will do with it that will return to you the greatest value. Put the plan into ACTION. But most importantly, MEASURE the results you achieve. You will not get it right the first time or every time. But keep practicing and you will get better.
- Manage the risks to your money as well. What can go wrong, will go wrong. Recognize that fact and you can plan for it too. Or at least prepare for it enough that even if life hurts you, it won't kill you. Life is full of risks. Be pro-active in recognizing them so that you can manage them too.
- Your income is your most valuable asset, in terms of its net present value for all your future years. Ensure it by making judicious use of insurance products, the least amount

for the shortest time, but enough for when it is really needed.

- Invest as much as you can as soon as you can. However you make your cash flow today, you want assets to produce enough cash flow for the quality of life you want in the future, when you decide to "End Work".
- Investments have risks just like your earned income cash flow. Manage those risks by balancing, diversifying, consistent deposits and even by using insurance products.
- Want an example? The Canada Pension Plan today is professionally managed. Its portfolio is a model for risk-managing investors in choosing your own investments.
- Quit lending the government your money, interest free. Apply the four Ds to pay as little as possible as late as possible, which may need some professional advice to keep everything legal.

Using a financial advisor

You will still need technical advice and support. Do not develop "advisor anxiety". If it is reluctance to share personal information, think of your doctor; your advisor is looking after your financial health. Your complete disclosure will help her do a better job. Money and sex are the most emotionally charged subjects we have to deal with. The reason for anxiety may be similar – guilt. Don't be ashamed, everyone wants sex and no one handles their money as well as they should. Get over it. You will never get financial planning – or sex – right, just keep practicing!

Advisor anxiety can be caused by fear of some salesman "selling" you something you do not fully understand, especially if the financial advisor is pressuring you by appealing to guilt. That is why you have read this book. You now understand the big picture and the fundamental choices. Your advisor is secondary, to help you with the technical details. Keep the strategic decisions for yourself. And pay her by the hour.

Putting it all into practice

You are twenty-five, finished an education, developed a trade, travelled and have landed your first real job with a decent company doing something you like; you are ready to get serious. Your $4000 gross nets out to about $3000 take-home. Besides taxes, your deductions include CPP and a group plan with $50,000 life insurance, short and long term disability and health and dental. That's a pretty good start. Let's say your CPP, company pension and group plan are taking 10% of your gross so paying yourself first may only need $300 a month of your net pay.

"Hang on", you say, what about paying off my student loans? Remember behavioural economics. It may be more rational to pay off all debt first but people including you (and me) are not rational. But we are creatures of habit. Get in the habit right from the start of putting that 10% of your net into providing your future income & independence. Invest as much as you can as early as you can.

Right now, your group insurance would be enough for your executors (likely your folks, get in the habit of having a will early too) in looking after your "final expenses", but if you expect to have a family, buy some term just to insure your insurability. Your odds of collecting are minimal (like the lottery) so it is cheap. $500,000 for a ten year term for a non-smoking male is only $27.60/month.

That leaves almost $275 to start investing. Some planners will suggest you are young enough to have a longer term risk horizon so you should throw it all into an aggressive equity fund. I prefer to start practicing balance and diversification from the start.

And don't forget tax planning as well. Put $100 every month into a balanced growth fund in an RRSP. That actually only takes $70 of your $300 after tax budget, with the tax deferral benefit at a 30% MTR and depositing your tax refund as well. Put another $100 of the after tax net into a fixed income fund within a TFSA, where the tax on interest income will be sheltered. That will also be your savings/emergency fund that you want to build up. You are left with $100 after tax for investing outside tax registered investments. This money you use for the more volatile third of your portfolio in an equity fund where dividends and capital gains get preferred tax treatment anyway so there is less advantage in registering it. And remember the tax sheltering and risk management advantages of insured "seg" funds for this portion.

Allocating at least 10% of your net to saving/investing right away is not just psychological. We have already discussed the importance of time (and Einstein) as being the key to financial independence. An example: at 25, Ted starts putting $100/month into a balanced fund, even at only 5% average return, he will have $152,602 at age 65. Bob pays off student loans first, and the wedding, and the kids, and the LOC taken for the house purchase to avoid the CMHC tax, and doesn't start on his own investment plan till age 45. To catch up to Ted, he deposits $200 a month to age 65. Both will have invested the same $48,000 but Bob's account will only be $82,206, only a bit better than half of Ted's who only saved half the monthly debit but started sooner. That Einstein, eh?!

At thirty you find your life partner and by thirty-five have a $300,000 mortgage and two ankle-biters. But you are now making $6000/month, netting $4000 at a 33.25% MTR. But because you started at 25, you were able to cash out your TFSA and a chunk of your RRSP under the Home Buyer Plan for your 20% down payment so you avoided the CMHC $10,000 tax (when "insurance" is mandated by government, it is a tax). You sit down with your partner to re-set your financial plan.

How much insurance do you need now? for how long? Besides final expenses, you now have a mortgage and a dependency period of twenty years till the kids are (hopefully) on their own. With no mortgage, you determine that the surviving partner would need about $2000 a month for child care and RESPs (a source of free money you will also want to take advantage of), or about half of your current take-home. Go back to the Table on page 70 about how much capital produces how much for how long at what rate. $100,000 at 5% would last twenty years with $8020 annual draw down. So replacing the $2000 a month of your income that your partner needs would take $300,000. Add the mortgage and final expenses and you need $650,000 to replace the portion of your income that your partner will need if you are gone. Oh, and maybe you should cover that $50,000 investment loan you took for starting a business on the side (the $80,000 equity in your home provided the double coverage).

But what about that cancer scare you had last year, and the sky-diving hobby you took up at 28? Oh yeah, you bought that cheap term insurance at 25, so no problem. And your group benefit plan for your new management position allows you to opt for up to three times salary. So $500,000 personal term insurance, renewed as a T20, and $216,000 on your group plan should suffice. Even though your mortgage is amortized over 30 years, you plan to add payments when you can (like your annual bonus) to pay it off in less than twenty. Except for Mr. Murphy, you could actually be on a Freedom 55 plan! Your Term 20 $500,000 plan is still only going to cost you $40/mo. Now you have $400 after tax to pay yourself, where should the extra $100 go? right into an RESP for the kids.

Now you are 45, well into middle management and making almost 100 grand, let's say $8000/mo. for round numbers, and getting up there in a 43.4% MTR. You have kept up your RRSP in balanced funds and used your TFSA for your fixed income assets. Add in your company pension and you are doing OK on the investment side, but what about the protection side?

The ten years remaining on your half million term insurance should now be more than you need. The mortgage should be half paid off and there are only ten years left on the kids' dependency needs. Insurance is flexible, you could always reduce your coverage. But the kids are morphing into teenagers (don't worry, they turn back into human beings in another ten years or so). And they have picked up expensive habits like hockey or ballet – and of course you want to do everything you can for the next Karen Kain or Wayne Gretzky. Oh, and you used the home equity Line of Credit to finance an addition. Good thing you took the level term coverage instead of the decreasing term option your advisor had told you about. Good thing your group plan has grown with your salary to compensate for inflation. So you have enough protection, and the remaining ten years is probably long enough too.

But you are now about half way through this journey we call life, and you may be starting to sense your own mortality. What about critical illness? long term care? a legacy for your kids (or your alma mater)? Because you have paid yourself first for twenty years, and because you pay your advisor by the hour and not on commission, she suggests that your $50,000 TFSA account would allow you to self-insure the critical illness risk; it is really just another form of "emergency" that you earmark that fund for. This would be a good time to start your own insurance company. Take the extra $200 of your 10% net and buy a universal life tax sheltered investment. If insurability is still an issue, just convert $100,000 of the term.

Mr. Murphy has spared you the worst and at 55 you are actually pretty financially independent. You have at least thirty more years and maybe forty. The kids are finishing school and setting off on their own journeys. Independence will give you the option of starting another journey if you wish. Start your own business, take a sabbatical to write a book. Perhaps you have nursed a special interest all these years. Your career has been satisfying and has provided the means to continue your special interest part-time. Now you could do it full-time. And it is not too late to be a rock musician, look at Mick and Keith!

There may be one problem with this happy plan. You may already be 35, or 45, when you are reading this book. No problem, the steps are the same. You may just have to save more or take more risk. Or like the New Yorker cartoon, take a later retirement. Whether you have otherwise been enjoying the journey of life, or recovering from life's setbacks, with today's lifespans, even Freedom 70 is not unreasonable.

Keep it in perspective

You do have better things to do in your life than financial planning. It really is not the most important thing. Number one in life is having someone to love. Cherish and support your family. An investment in love pays the greatest dividends. Your second priority is your health. Work at it. Your body can take a lot of abuse until 40 or 45 when your neglect will start to show. However, if you work at it, and take care of yourself, you can maintain a good level of health and energy till 85 or so. Third, you need something to do, something to keep your mind active and engaged, that provides a sense of satisfaction as your return on the investment of your time and effort.

Financial planning comes in a distant fourth on your happiness priority list, mainly to facilitate pursuing the first three priorities.

You now know what you need to do to ensure your financial independence. I wish someone had told me all this forty years ago. I might be cruising around the world instead of writing this book. On the other hand, writing this book may have been more interesting. If I have not proven to be a very successful planner myself, I have been most fortunate in love, health and interesting things to do. I may not have all that I want but I certainly have all that I need.

“Those that can, do; those that can’t, teach”. Here endeth the lesson.

Start where you are. Use what you have. Do what you can. Arthur Ashe, American professional tennis player

A brief Bibliography

For those who may have become so enamoured of Financial Planning from my book that you are looking for further enlightenment in your financial literacy, here are the tomes from which I have stolen many ideas.

Chilton, David Barr (1998). *The Wealthy Barber - Everyone's common sense guide to becoming financially independent.* New York, Three Rivers Press

Christianson, David (2012). *Managing the Bull – Detect and Deflect the crap - A no-nonsense approach to personal finance.* Winnipeg, Knowledge Bureau Inc.

Ford, Donald A. (2000). *Don't Sell Yourself Short! - A slightly irreverent guide to personal financial success.* Ottawa, Heney Lake Holdings Inc.

Nelson, Douglas V. (Third Edition 2014). *Master Your Retirement - How to fulfill your dreams with peace of mind.* Winnipeg, Knowledge Bureau Inc.

A good head and a good heart are always a formidable combination. -- Nelson Mandela, former South African president

Acknowledgements

I have just spent five years in the financial advice business. My research for this book has been learning today's financial planning practices from the worm's eye view. I lost the million dollar business I had been planning to sell for a comfy retirement. You might say my financial planning was not very well diversified. After trying another start-up, consulting and some odd jobs, I was recruited to sell insurance. I had actually spent a year in financial sales forty years before as a fresh Commerce grad. But back then, when I was able to get a job in the industry that did turn me on, I realized my heart really wasn't into finance. This time, after an interesting and varied career in the aviation industry, I decided I was ready for something completely different. But to paraphrase George Santayana: *Those that do not learn from their mistakes are doomed to repeat them.* I have again concluded that finance, insurance and investments, interesting subjects though they may be, do not light my fires.

There are several people whom I need to thank for their role in my late career in financial planning. The Richardsons of World Financial Group welcomed me, and I enjoyed their enthusiastic cabal. But once I decided that the WFG business model was not for me, I left abruptly without a proper goodbye and thank-you for their efforts, including to my "upline", Nardia.

Charlie Burns and his gang at PPI Solutions in Winnipeg provided the professional environment I was seeking and always treated me very well; Ed Misurka surely felt some frustration trying to complete my supervision requirements for licensing.

Buzz Grant of Mortgage Logic gave me an office and a clientele. There are very few who will give a senior a chance to start over. And that is what the financial services business has given me, a chance to start over.

And then there are a few dozen very nice people who have trusted my advice, in helping me make a living the past five years. I trust that I gave you full value.

There is an axiom in aviation: "Learn from the mistakes of others; you will not live long enough to make them all yourself". My principal qualification to write this book is that I have lived long enough that I have made them all myself. Sharing what I have learned may save you from a few. I'm going flying.

If more of us valued food and cheer and song above hoarded gold, it would be a merrier world. -- J.R.R. Tolkien, British writer

If you enjoyed this little tome, watch for

SHELL GAME - understanding public finance

Chapter xx The Income Inequality Challenge

Mrs. Left says everyone needs a reasonable level of income, to escape from poverty. "Our wealthy nation can afford it, it is the least we (the better off) can do".

Mr. Right says: "Get a job! Pull yourself up by your boot-straps". Even Mrs. Left agrees with Mr. Right that a job is the best solution to poverty. "We just need to create a new universal jobs program". We *could call it "employment insurance" (not unemployment insurance as that is poor packaging – and, yes, that was sarcasm*). Mr. Right says "No way, that will need an army of bureaucrats to administer" (*how many people work for EI anyway?*). "But", says Mrs. Left, "how can the poor pick themselves up by the bootstraps unless they have a pair of boots?"

Ms. Centre, listening attentively, suggests: "But we already have the army of bureaucrats, they are called the Canada Revenue Agency; why don't they work in reverse, distributing boots, then taking back half the straps the people make with them?" "But how much do boots cost Ms. Centre? We couldn't afford boots for everyone." "Why not?", offers Ms. Centre, the 90% of people who already have boots are just going to pay for them right back in their regular taxes."

"So what you are suggesting is a negative income tax," says Mr. Right, "there are just way too many questions to take that risk. Most people would just live on the dole, like they do now." "That is a terrible prejudice" stomps Mrs. Left, "people do not want to be poor. It is the 100% claw back you put on their first pair of straps that kills any incentive."

"Actually folks", interjects Ms. Centre, "those questions were all answered in the MinCome experiment in Dauphin Manitoba in the 1970s. It actually worked well. People kept working and they even found kids stayed in school longer and families stayed together more." "OK Ms. Smart, I mean, Centre, tell us how it would work".

"Well, just like the tax system, except money flows both ways. Instead of a personal exemption before one starts paying tax, every adult gets $1000 a month. Everyone then starts paying tax from the first dollar they make, from any source." But $12,000 a year is barely better than welfare" objects Mrs. Left, "the LICO (low-income-cut-off, definition of poverty) is $28,000 for a family of four." Hold on Ms. Centre adds, "Two adults, and applying a child tax credit, say $200 a month per child, and that family will have an income better than $28,000."

"Back up Ms. Centre", demands Mr. Right, "when does the government get its $12,000 back from Mr. Poorman?" "That depends on the tax rate" answers Ms. Centre. The current marginal rate for a person in Manitoba (Ms. Centre's home province) is 25.8% up to $31,465 taxable income; it goes up to 27.75% above that to $45,916; at $45,454 earned income, Mr. Poorman will have paid back the $12,000 negative income tax he had received monthly. A higher tax rate of say 33% would pay it all back at $36,000 earned income. The negative and positive income taxes could be kept revenue neutral to the government. But keep in mind that revenue neutral would include absorbing other indirect taxes like EI premiums and even CPP, since the negative income tax would continue into retirement, not to mention the "savings" from administering it all by a computer."

"While if you can keep it revenue neutral, I can almost buy into the idea" says Mr. Right, but why not take it a step further and have a flat tax for everyone?" "Now you really are going too far Mr. Right," chimes in Mrs. Left. "I can accept using a negative income tax to provide everyone a decent living standard, but progressive tax rates, where the rich who can afford more, pay more, is the holy grail of our social democracy."

"OK", backs down Mr. Right, "I can see where that may be too much for the bleeding hearts to accept, even with universal welfare. But working men and women are never going to accept paying all the Poormans of the world for not working."

"While now we are down to a marketing problem", adds Ms. Centre. Let me suggest how we might package this income redistribution to make it more acceptable to current tax payers. Let's call it a job creation program. But instead of giving money to bureaucrats for programs, we will pay people to create their own job. A minimum job would be 25 hours a week at the minimum wage of $10/hour: What do you know, that is about $1000/month."

The robots are killing jobs faster than ever, but I believe there is no end of worthwhile jobs to do. More people could start day care centres. Did you notice we just solved government's number one challenge, unemployment? We have just created full employment, everyone has a job!" Eliminating poverty is just a side benefit.

"It sounds a little too slick to me", says Mr. Right, "my people are going to have a lot of questions ..." "And my people are never going to trust the program is not going to screw Mr. Poorman in some other way" adds Mrs. Left.

"That's OK", answers Ms. Centre, "I can write a book about it."

If you want to make enemies, try to change something.
--Woodrow Wilson, 28th U.S. president

Made in the USA
Monee, IL
04 November 2026

67387517R00075